M. BET

Author of *Done L*
and Acqu...... ....egration

MW00719981

CHANGE

Happens

SECOND EDITION ——

Your Guide to Navigating Change
Using the 5C Model

M. Beth Page
Published by Authenticity Press
Copyright © 2011, 2020 by M. Beth Page
First Edition: April 2011
Second Edition: August 2020

Editing: Phyllis Kennelly and Shanaya Nelson
Original cover design: Chantal Gabriell
Interior layout: Chantal Gabriell & Simeon Goa

Printed and bound in the USA

Authenticity Press website address: www.authenticitypress.com

Page, M. Beth, 1964-
Change happens : your guide to navigating change using the 5C Model
Second Edition / M. Beth Page.

Includes bibliographical references.
2011: ISBN 978-0-9739130-4-0
2020: ISBN 978-0-9739130-5-7

     1. Organizational change--Management. I. Title.

HD58.8.P33 2011   658.4'06   C2011-901511-0

Testimonials for *Change Happens*

"As leaders in 2020, we are being called upon to lead in unprecedented times. We are experiencing change that is challenging us as individuals, families, organizations, and society. As we rise to meet these challenges, we need to access practical wisdom.

Dr. Beth Page has created a wonderful change leadership resource for us all. *Change Happens* is insightful, fun and provides an amazing change leadership framework. You are going to love the clear and straightforward 5C change model that will guide you step-by-step through change. As we are called upon to lead change with compassion, empathy, and vision; *Change Happens* is a must in your resource library."

–Mark Fulton
Founder and CEO LeadingCulture

"*Change Happens* provides a simple yet deep perspective on guiding change. As Beth demonstrates very clearly, people are frustrated when change is 'done to them.' This is a common, and often deserved, criticism of international aid work. The 5C Model brings the human dimension of change to the center of focus. From Azerbaijan to Zimbabwe, I can use Beth's framework to honor the current culture while facilitating trans-organizational, system-wide change that is embraced and led by empowered individuals. Whether engaging employees or citizens, you will find this book a trustworthy companion on your adventure."

–William Sparks,
Senior Advisor, International Aid Organization

"This practical, engaging book offers a clear path to leading change in organizations. Enlivened by examples from practice, and grounded in relevant theory, *Change Happens* invites readers to see the possibilities for creating collaborative, intentional change processes. The book offers self-assessment questions, guiding principles, and action steps, all of which are designed to help readers readily apply the tools in their own contexts. Beyond steps and strategies, the 5C Model is deeply infused with respect, safety and honouring. In short, people matter. This is a toolkit with heart."

–Dr. Rhonda L. Margolis,
Certified Executive Coach, Principal, RLM Learning Innovations Inc

"Change Happens is written in a style that is engaging and respectful of the reader. It is condensed yet full of easy to digest information, presented in a conversational, inclusive tone. It provides awareness, provokes thought and stimulates connection to your workplace. And just when you come to appreciate that you could use some help, the tools appear that invite you to formulate a practical, conscious map to successful change implementation and a sustained positive workplace."

–W Wawrysh, Broadcasting Industry,
HR Manager

"Change Happens provides a treasure chest of research and experience-based advice using a definitive framework to help leaders navigate the challenges of change. Many unique observations and clearly defined goals, which once revealed to the reader are instantly seen as essential. Keeping with her respectful style, Beth guides you through a myriad of options to complement your needs and interests. The answers are contained within, so enjoy the read."

–Gina M Donaldson, Global Consulting Firm, Senior Managing Consultant,
Strategy and Transformation

"In Change Happens: Your Guide to Navigating Change Using the 5C Model, Beth explains each dimension of her 5C Model in a clear and succinct manner. She presents reflective questions and action steps to empower us to lead a successful change initiative. Beth honors the employees by bringing them into the change initiative early and she keeps them actively engaged throughout the process. Change Happens is as important to leaders as it is to HR professionals, consultants and employees. Beth eloquently inspires us to improve our competency, productivity, and success when it comes to change initiatives. As a student of Beth's while pursuing my MA in Leadership, I have seen Beth live the lessons she provides in Change Happens. These lessons are lived in a spirit of inquiry while honoring others and encouraging them to be fully engaged. "

–Jean Hankel, MA, Canadian Oil and Gas Industry, HR-Learning Transfer

Dedication

This book is dedicated to my family:
my parents, Barbara and Carl Page
my brother, Michael Page
my nephews, Alex and Shawn
Thank you for your love and support.

About the Author

Beth Page provides organization development consulting and coaching services in collaboration with her clients. Beth is the president of Dream Catcher Consulting, a firm dedicated to working with organizations to navigate change and renewal by leveraging the value of the human dimension with achievement of superior business results. A few of her clients have included: the Children's Hospital in Denver, Colorado; the University of Victoria; the BC Public Service Agency and Royal Roads University.

Beth is an associate faculty member with the School of Leadership Studies at Royal Roads University, and teaches in the graduate certificate in Strategic Human Resources Management and the Graduate Certificate in Change Management. She also teaches in the Master of Arts in Leadership.

She completed her PhD at the University of Victoria. She also has a Master of Science degree in organization development from Pepperdine University, and a Master of Science in college student personnel from Western Illinois University. She is a professional certified coach with the International Coach Federation and holds her Certified Professional Human Resources (CPHR) designation. She is accredited to administer the Resilience @ Work assessment and she is a certified Emotional Intelligence coach with the EQ in Action Profile. Beth has also completed the Advanced Human Resources Management program at the University of Toronto, the Certificate in Management Development from the School of Business at Carleton University, and a Bachelor of Arts degree in psychology at Carleton University.

She is the author of *Done Deal: Your Guide to Merger and Acquisition Integration* and contributed to the book *Awakening the Workplace: Achieving Connection, Fulfillment and Success at Work.*

Acknowledgments

This book would not have been as enriching without the ancestral land to nourish me as I have written, worked and learned on these lands. I am grateful to this land and the ancestral families who have stewarded it for generations. I wish to acknowledge the ancestral, traditional, and unceded Indigenous territories of the Halalt, Penelakut, and Stz'uminus peoples where I reside on Vancouver Island, British Columbia, Canada.

I am grateful to many people who supported me during my writing of Change Happens. Thank you for your support.

I cherish my clients who have included me in their change and integration work. I continue to be amazed by the capacity for change that is possible when employees are involved and invited to work with the leaders in the organization. I have witnessed many partnerships unfold with the involvement of employees. Thousands of workshop participants have influenced and shaped the material in *Change Happens*. Their enthusiasm for the 5C Model inspired me to keep writing.

I am grateful to Phyllis Kennelly. She is the first person who read *Change Happens* and helped bring order and clarity to my message. Our ongoing dialogue about the evolution of the model, and our partnership that began in 2002, have resulted in rich conversations. Her editing contributions enhanced the final product significantly.

I have been blessed by the generosity of Roger Harrison and Ron Short, two significant contributors to the field of organization development whom I have contacted throughout the years to access their advice. They have been wonderful sounding boards and I treasure the wisdom they have so readily shared with me. Roger died in 2015 and his legacy lives on in his family, friends, colleagues, and people like me who he mentored. I often find myself reminded of his wisdom while working with clients, as a result of the lessons he so generously shared with me. As a way to continue to honor his legacy of impact, I have left the foreward Roger wrote for to the first edition of *Change Happens*. I am also delighted to include the foreward written by Jan Johnson and Ronald Short for the second edition.

My communities of practice, specifically the OD Café that meets quarterly in Victoria, have been wonderful sources of support and encouragement. My colleagues have provided input as the model has continued to develop and they have been instrumental in nurturing its evolution. My students keep me on my learning edge. Their questions and their passion challenge me to keep learning, as both an educator and a lifelong learner.

I am indebted to Dawn Brown, a dear friend and author, who always had words of wisdom and encouragement for me. Susan Atkinson, Kathy Bishop, Joni Campbell, Michelle Clement, Mary Eshenko, Catherine Etmanski, Sarah Evans, Jim Flood, Sheila Flood, Teara Fraser, Mark Fulton, Chantal Gabriell, Tammy Hoffman, Laura Jackson, Doris Kiiffner, Mel MacLeod, Rhonda Margolis, Louise McDonald, Daniel Nelson, Louise Oliphant, Bruce Oliphant, Lynda Pedley, Pam Renney, Joanna Runnells, Peter Schoonbeek, Vicki Schoonbeek, Leslie Smith, Micki Stirling, Wendy Wawrysh, and Tony Williams offered their encouragement throughout the project. A special note of thanks to Theresa Bell and the librarians at Royal Roads University for their help and support during the final phase of research.

Chantal Gabriell completed the cover art and Simeon Goa completed the interior layout. Thanks to Shanaya Nelson who provided her professional editing expertise. I am grateful to each of you for your professionalism, wonderful sense of timing and enthusiasm for the book.

To the many friends and family members who believed in me, thank you for cheering me on.

Foreword to the First Edition by Roger Harrison

I have known Beth Page for a good number of years now, and it gives me a great deal of pleasure to have been asked to write this Foreword. This is a book I could wish I had written myself. It is a book dedicated to excellence in the practice of my own chosen profession, by a highly experienced organization development consultant who is also a fine writer and a passionate learner. Beth's dedication to learning stands out on almost every page, but particularly in the way she weaves her own insights into what she has learned from others.

It is always a delight to me when someone who knows consulting in its day-to-day practice writes a book that is not only informed by that practice, but is also grounded in solid theory. By no means all of us are able to translate the intuition, personal style, and "feel" that are such an important part of our stock in trade into practical and sensible guidance for others. In *Change Happens*, Beth has succeeded admirably in doing just that. Her writing is clear and concise, and Beth presents material that is truly complex in an organized, step-by-step form that makes it accessible.

In *Change Happens*, Beth addresses the daunting task of planning and implementing significant organizational change by the use of a deceptively simple framework that she calls "The 5Cs," namely Communication, Confidentiality, Cultural Compatibility, Courtship and Completion. This framework encloses and organizes a truly diverse and comprehensive wealth of theory, experience, anecdotes, and cases, all leavened by a substantial amount of common sense.

The book is laid out in straightforward order, considering each of the 5Cs in turn, and then look at what happens when these change, imperatives are ignored or insufficiently implemented. The major points are liberally illustrated with examples from Beth's own practice, and with quotations and references to others' work. I especially admire the way that Beth has learned from other writers in the field, and how she both honors their achievements and integrates their insights into her own theory and practice. While rich in her own thought and experience, Beth is never so wrapped up in her own ego that she sleights or ignores what she owes to those many others toiling in our field. The result is a book that brings together in a very pragmatic way Beth's own insights, together with the best practices of working consultants and change managers as they have evolved over the years.

Having myself written both early and extensively on organization culture, as well as engaging in attempts to change it, I very much appreciate Beth's sensible treatment of the Cultural Compatibility aspect of the change process. Given that culture change initiatives invariably evoke significant resistance, her strong emphasis on honoring and building upon the current organization culture is both wise and parsimonious— why make trouble for ourselves by trampling roughshod on the cherished values and customs of members of the organization, when culture change is so challenging at the best of times?

I also greatly appreciate the emphasis placed in *Change Happens* on the importance of building trust through frequent straightforward communication on the part of change managers. It is so very easy when making one's way through the minefield that major organization change can become to believe that we are sparing others the anxiety and uncertainty we ourselves are carrying by shielding them from bad news or ambiguity. Beth unmasks those fantasies in no uncertain terms, showing how very short sighted they are, if not actually cynically self-serving.

In similar fashion, the idea that a change process belongs to the change managers is neatly put to rest in the section on Courtship, where

Beth makes a strong case for continuously involving all levels of an organization in the change, and giving them ownership of it. It is so easy for those involved in planning and implementing change to talk mostly to one another and become isolated from the rest of the organization. I have myself certainly learned through bitter experience the importance of continuously promoting a change project through dialogue with organizational members at all levels, not only telling and selling, but willingly listening to points of view that we may not care to hear.

Although the book is certainly complete in itself, there is a great deal of material for further study that is referenced and pointed to in the references and in the section on internet resources. This book could certainly serve very adequately as the central text in a course on organization change, as well as belonging on the desk of anyone who is given responsibility for planning and/or implementing change. In today's world, that means most of us.

In sum, I very much like this book. It leaves no matter of importance to change managers unaddressed, yet it is compact enough to be a fairly quick read. When you have read it once, I feel sure that you will be drawn to refer to it again and again as you practice its lessons in the course of your own work. I hope that you will find it as useful and informative as I have.

Roger Harrison, author of *Consultant's Journey: A Dance of Work and Spirit*

Foreward to the Second Edition
by Jan Johnson & Ronald Short

Change Happens is clear, easy to read, and put to immediate use. It outlines a thorough framework along with a succinct and applicable process for a wide scope of organizations from very small to large multinational companies. The overall theme in the model is intentionally engaging both the heart and head. This is reflected in each chapter, and each of the 5C dimensions. Specifically, the model provides a clear and powerful framework which provides guidance and direction to clients throughout the change process. Several examples and ideas are provided that invite the reader to explore what strategies fit their unique needs within the context of the 5C framework.

The theory and practice methods are based on Beth's experiences, and what she has learned over many years of guiding clients through step by step processes to support them. A depth of information is shared with each element of the 5C model. Precise methods are presented along with clear supporting theory including her practical experience with clients. This book shares logical information and presents the 5Cs in an easy to read and apply model.

The reader will benefit from both successes and failures. Problem areas with descriptive behaviors are explored along with specific actions to mitigate these potential issues. Methods others can learn from are shared throughout. She also generously features and quotes multiple senior professionals in the field, adding their learnings to her own experience.

Communication is identified as one of the crucial 5C steps. It is essential and reflected throughout the 5C model, and in each step of the process. This includes communication with all shareholders, including board members, executives, managers, and employees throughout the organization. This book also offers guidance in how to effectually communicate in general, as well as sharing specific guidance on what communication will most likely be successful in reaching multiple stakeholders. Additional guidance is offered on individual types of statements that can reduce trust and commitment at any point and any level within the change process along with recommendations on what will strengthen trust amidst change.

To support change practitioners and leaders throughout the change process, critical questions are introduced for each of the 5Cs. These critical questions apply to any change process and are offered to amplify key areas of focus as change occurs. For change practitioners that are seeking to avoid the pitfalls of change, a listing of indicators that may interfere or significantly negatively impact the process are identified as the counter Cs. These counter Cs give clarity to specific behaviors that may cause problems. This is easy and clear and can be used as a guide to all involved in the change process.

We appreciated the list of behaviors that are commonly experienced at each step and can derail the entire process. This serves as a guide for leaders to know, understand, and watch for negative behaviors that can disrupt the change effort. It can be used as a check list for leaders and managers to guide their observations and their responses.

As mentioned earlier, the key is using the head and the heart. This is the overriding theme throughout Beth's book, with a clear demonstration of the critical importance of each element of the 5Cs. If you are seeking to engage both the heads and the hearts of your employees amidst change, the 5C model will support you in this effort.

Jan Johnson, author, *The EQ Fitness Handbook*
Ron Short, author, *Learning in Relationship*

Notice to Readers

The information in this book is offered as an aid to developing and maintaining professional competence, with the understanding that the author and publisher are not providing legal or other professional advice. Exercise your professional judgment about the correctness and applicability of the material. The author, publisher and vendor make no representation or warranties regarding the outcome or the use to which the information in this book is put and are not assuming any liability for any claims, losses or damages arising out of the use of this book.

Table of Contents

Preface

Change Happens is a result of almost 20 years of research and work with the 5C Model. The original research that yielded the 5C Model was explored in my first book, *Done Deal*. Over the past several years, work with clients has continued to expand the application of the 5C Model. Mike Maughlin, a colleague and client, ordered copies of *Done Deal* for his organization and then invited me to help him and his colleagues apply the 5C Model in the healthcare organization where he worked. Thanks to this invitation, I was able to see firsthand how the model worked for integration and change projects that weren't in the traditional field of merger and acquisition integration. My clients have continued to invite me to be a partner in applying the model.

As I shared the model with colleagues, I was encouraged to "see" beyond the original application of the model and apply it to a variety of change initiatives. As I reconnected with clients, I began to discover that once again my clients were teaching me. The model was embedded in their organizations as a change model. The managers found the model easy to use and easy to replicate. It provided a shared language for discussing the status of change initiatives and determining next steps for continuing to embed the change more fully within the organization. In essence, the model was helping clients look at their organization as a system and apply integrated thinking to their change initiatives. As a result of our work together and their trust in me, I have learned new ways to use the model to help organizations be more successful with their change and integration efforts.

The 5C Model has evolved and grown. In addition to the classic and foundational material that informed the original research, *Change*

Happens has new material, tools for practical application and web links to additional online resources to support your change efforts.

Join me in *Change Happens* as we continue to apply the 5C Model in service of organizations and employees to create more successful change efforts that truly leverage the value of the human dimension.

In this second edition of *Change Happens*, I have incorporated new material to provide change practitioners and leaders alike with additional tools and helpful information. In light of the growing emphasis on resilience, a new chapter exploring the role of leadership sustainability amidst change has been added. Research in the area of values-based leadership is now more fully represented as a result of research I conducted. Material has been added throughout to reflect the learning that clients and I have continued to experience since the first edition of *Change Happens* was published. The references and Internet Resources sections have been updated to include additional reading and resources to support change practitioners in potential development areas. May this revised second edition of *Change Happens* continue to support you as you honor the human dimension amidst change.

Introduction

Change Happens is written for you if you have been dissatisfied with the outcomes of previous change experiences. Change management initiatives involving employees, managers, business unit leaders, shareholders, clients, customers and many other stakeholders recognize that the human dimension is vital for achieving business results.

Employees, supervisors and mid-level managers often feel that change is "done to them." They feel powerless, betrayed and sometimes out of control due to processes that result in significant changes to them and their work environment. This diminishes their sense of professional competency, loyalty to the organization and overall productivity.

The business leaders, human resources (HR) practitioners, organization development consultants, change management practitioners and managers that comprise the change management team must address the concerns and issues of the human dimension if the change is to positively impact the entire organization.

The 5C Model is a change framework that resulted from my research and work with clients as an organization development practitioner. The model focuses on five key dimensions of change: communication, confidentiality, cultural compatibility, courtship and completion. This 5C Model is designed to offer professionals a different, more integrated approach to change management. Incorporating the 5Cs will deepen your understanding of the change process and allow you to anticipate the impact, develop an action plan and act on it in a way that honors the human dimension of any organizational change initiative. The 5C Model will increase collaboration among all the stakeholders participating in, and affected by, the change. As one client put it, the 5C Model offers "a form of integrated thinking" for managers, practitioners and employees.

Part One

"The most successful species on the planet are those that continuously adapt to their changing environment."

—Richard Barrett

Chapter 1 • The 5C Model and Change

The 5C Model is available to you as a strategic model for strengthening the success of your change initiatives. Business leaders, clients and internal change management practitioners have consistently commented on the practicality of the model, and the ease of use. In this chapter, I offer an overview of the model and explain each of the five dimensions. As you are reviewing this material, I invite you to consider the following questions: What aspects of the 5C Model does our organization manage well? What aspects of the model could be applied to benefit our organization?

One of my clients described each of the dimensions of the model as levers and noted that, depending on the stage of the change initiative, different levers benefited from greater emphasis. The both/and opportunity here is to pay attention to both the activity being implemented while considering the best timing for implementing these activities. Ultimately, for change initiatives to be successful, you must actively emphasize each lever as needed. Ensure that your team acts upon each of the dimensions with intention. This will help organizations achieve integration of their change initiatives and experience greater success. Each of the chapters that follow will offer practical guidance and tools for exploring the dimensions more fully and applying them in your organization.

Ultimately, if you are seeking to navigate a change initiative that demonstrates respect for the employees, builds trust amidst the ambiguity of the change and invites employees to get involved and claim ownership of the change, then the 5C Model is available to you as a tool to serve you and your organization.

Let's begin with the 5C Model and a brief description of each of the dimensions:

Figure 1. The 5C Change Model

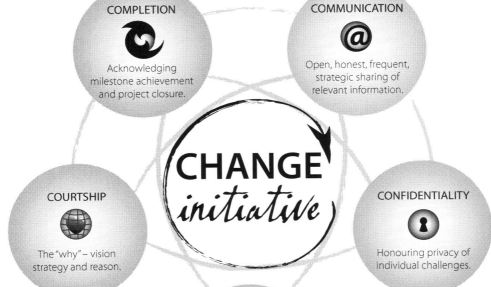

The 5C Model: Dimension 1
Communication

Communication is the open, honest, frequent and strategic sharing of relevant information. Take every opportunity to explain and talk about the change initiative because communication is vital throughout this entire process.

Change management practitioners include managers, internal consultants, HR business partners and business leaders. Emphasize the need for frequent meetings with all employees and other stakeholders to avoid any uncertainty. Buono and Bowditch (1989) advised managers avoid using "killer phrases" like "We will only tell employees something when there is something to tell. Information can always be shared." (p. 11) Larkin and Larkin (2006) went further and asserted,

> *Managing employee expectations requires early communi-*
> *cation. When you communicate very early, say in the first*
> *five days after a public announcement, employees expect an*
> *imprecise plan full of estimates, probabilities and contin-*
> *gencies. And that is what you deliver. When you delay the*
> *communication for four, six, eight, ten weeks, employees*
> *develop an extraordinarily high expectation of detail to be*
> *communicated. An expectation you will not meet.* (p. 13)

In a recent workshop with clients who were directly affected by a corporate public announcement, we learned that the 3 weeks following individual meetings with their managers had been lacking in follow-up communication. The leadership team was in "planning mode." When they were invited to attend a full-day workshop, the employees expected refined and specific details about the plan. When the information wasn't forthcoming, their disappointment and frustration were immediately apparent.

Personnel issues such as job security are uppermost in employees' minds in the initial days following the announcement of the change. The practice of open, honest communication ensures that employees' concerns about job security and their role in the organization are addressed up front. As Buono and Bowditch (1989) emphasized, "Organizational members are more likely to react positively when they are well informed, exposed to unfavorable as well as favorable possibilities, than when they are forced to rely on hearsay and speculation" (p. 11).

Communication figures heavily throughout the entire change management process. It provides employees and other constituents with valuable information and addresses the uncertainty that exists with any transition or change.

One complaint I have never heard from employees is that the organization "over-communicated." To grasp a new idea, new plan or new direction in a change initiative, employees need to hear the message repeatedly before it can be internalized and acted upon. Professional communications experts suggest that potential consumers need to hear a message five or more times before it gets noticed. Employees would benefit from the same frequency of communication when we are developing the communications plan.

What role does consistent communication play in building trust during change? In the Harvard Business Review article, "Enemies of Trust" Galford and Drapeau (2003) asserted, "The building blocks of trust are unsurprising: They're old-fashioned managerial virtues like consistency, clear communication and a willingness to tackle awkward questions" (p. 90). These authors went on to offer the following tips for addressing one of the more problematic issues for organizations—delivering inconsistent messages. Galford encouraged organizations to think through their priorities,

> *Before broadcasting priorities articulate them to yourself or a trusted advisor to ensure that they're coherent and that you're being honest with people instead of making unrealistic commitments. Make sure your managerial team communicates a consistent message. Reserve big-bang announcements for truly major initiatives.* (p. 91)

The 5C Model: Dimension 2
Confidentiality

Confidentiality is the foundation of trust for honoring and respecting private sharing of individual challenges. Respect for employees, managers, shareholders, customers and clients is paramount. We must respect the ideas, input, concerns and fears expressed by all stakeholders. For many stakeholders, expression offers release and facilitates resolution of the issue. Change management practitioners demonstrate respect through listening to ideas; listening to all stakeholders leads to release and facilitates change. Honoring the issues that get raised during change is one key strategy for engaging the support of employees to facilitate the change initiative. At its core, respecting confidentiality of individual issues strengthens trust.

"What happens in Vegas, stays in Vegas" is a mantra used by HR practitioners who work on the front line with employees expressing concerns during change. Often, employees don't want to be perceived as not being supportive of the change with their managers, so they raise their concerns with other employees or with the HR practitioner. Being able to coach and support employees expressing these concerns will help employees feel safe about expressing their uncertainty and fears in an environment of ambiguity. One of the key benefits of this dimension is the recognition that some conversations are intended to be private dialogues between two professionals—one helping another navigate the internal transition process. The support and coaching received during these meetings can help employees understand their individual roles in the change. They begin to gain a better understanding of the bigger picture, and get their individual concerns and questions answered. Also, the privacy of these meetings, and knowing that the information shared will remain private, are vital to strengthening trust between the employee and the organization. These conversations—where employees learn that they matter as people, that their issues matter and that their concerns are heard and respected—are critical. Business leaders are encouraged to partner with their HR staff early in the change initiative by sharing information and planning. When this type of sharing partnership is absent, the unintended consequence is a lost opportunity for supporting the change. The organization, HR, and employees benefit when planning information is shared among stakeholders.

We need to remind ourselves that there is an element of loss that occurs as employees make change. Individuals experience loss when a fellow employee's promotion or unexpected departure occurs, or a mentor or more senior employee retires or moves to another organization. Employees who relied on the wisdom and guidance of these individuals are affected.

The 5C Model: Dimension 3
Cultural Compatibility

Cultural Compatibility is the degree of values alignment, core beliefs and guiding principles of an organization. Dennison (1990) stated an organization's culture consists of "the underlying values, beliefs and principles that define an organization's management system, as well as the management practices and behavior that reinforce those principles" (p. 2). A number of credible cultural assessment tools such as cultural surveys and facilitated focus groups are available. Utilize them to inform decision makers and change management practitioners about the cultural differences and areas of alignment among different departments and lines of business in the organization.

A more detailed definition of organizational culture comes from Dr. Edgar Schein (1984), who defined culture as "the pattern of basic assumptions a given group has invented, discovered or developed while learning to cope with its problems of external adaptation and internal integration" (p. 3). The assumptions, Schein noted, will "be taught to new members as the correct way to perceive, think and feel in relation to those problems" (p. 3).

As Schein (1983) pointed out, the challenge of assessing an organization's culture "is more a matter of surfacing assumptions which will be recognizable once they have been uncovered" (p. 17). Identifying cultural compatibility on such core values as ethics, collaboration, sharing of information and respect is an important consideration in the assessment of culture as part of the overall change.

Subcultures within organizations are prevalent even among different departments that are part of the same line of business. If you have ever moved between two departments in an organization, you have experienced the subtle and not so subtle cultural differences.

The impact of not assessing the degree of cultural compatibility might have significant consequences; cultural tensions and clashes can cause problems, as Buono and Bowditch (1989) emphasized. Cultural compatibility emphasizes the importance of assessing the culture of all the departments involved in a change project. Many change initiatives are designed to link and integrate departments and when the assessment and active management of cultural compatibility is lacking, significant issues can emerge.

The 5C Model: Dimension 4
Courtship

Courtship is the "why" of this change initiative—the vision, strategy and reason. Collaboration doesn't occur easily; it needs a courtship period, one that involves all stakeholders. Bring together executives, managers, change management practitioners, HR and employees to tackle a particular problem, model the value of courtship for the organization and ensure that a diversity of perspectives will be represented. As Raelin (2018) observed, "Leadership in the current knowledge era cannot rely on a single source of expertise; rather it needs to be a collaborative practice" (p. 66). As leaders seek to actively engage employees in change, collaboration may offer a path forward. When it comes to working in organizations with challenging issues that she referred to as messes, Armson (2011) reminded us, "Learning our way through is the only way to make progress without making it worse. Quick fixes will not work because the problem and the priorities are unclear. Instead, I try to look for improvements rather than solutions" (Loc. 17). Who knew that inadvertently, our problem-solving-oriented selves may be making situations worse? What might be possible if we focused on identifying improvements in collaboration with the people around us and actively "courted" their input?

If mediocrity and complacency permeate the environment, courtship may be the way to plant the seed of change and increase collaboration. It is during this beginning stage that the work of engaging individuals gets underway. Then and only then will employees begin to see the need for their involvement and support the change.

When speaking with employees about change, "sell, don't tell." This is a critical leadership skill. Leaders must engage people's hearts and minds and inspire them to join the organization in the change initiative. John Kotter (1996) defined leadership as coping with change: "The problem for us today is that stability is no longer the norm. And most experts agree that over the next few decades, the environment will become only more volatile" (p. 15). For example, Vail (as cited in Buono & Nurick, 1992) used the metaphor of "permanent whitewater" (p. 26) to characterize modern organizations. Many specific forces act as stimulants for change, including the changing nature of the workforce, technology, economic shocks, social trends, world politics, global pandemics and competition. With the global impact of climate change, banking deregulation, food safety and health, the rate and pace of change continue to accelerate. Leaders who can help their employees move through the "permanent whitewater" of change recognize the importance of involving employees as partners and collaborators.

The 5C Model: Dimension 5
Completion

Completion is the acknowledgment of achieving ongoing milestones and intentional closure for the project. Completion emphasizes the importance of celebrating achievement and helping employees to take a moment to honor and recognize what has been accomplished before moving forward with the next project. Too often, organizations move from project to project, leaving employees change-weary and craving time to honor the completion of each project. This is a time in our history when organizations ask members to reflect their relentless focus on the next initiative. The consequence is that we are robbing ourselves of our present moment experience and the opportunity to honor and celebrate completion. I refer to this tendency as living in the chronic next spiral. It's no wonder our employees and organizations are feeling a collective sense of exhaustion as they think, "Not another change!"

As change agents, business leaders, and project managers, we need to build room into our planning process for measuring our success and our achievement, and acknowledging completion by taking time to celebrate. One of the key messages offered by William Bridges (2003), in his book *Managing Transitions*, is that without endings there are no new beginnings. The organization has a responsibility to create space for completion, so the ending of one project can be acknowledged before moving on to the "next" initiative, project or change.

A key strategy for achieving completion and helping all levels of the organization monitor progress is to establish 90-day plans. Initially,

I articulated a need for 100-day plans as a best practice. However, many organizations are driving toward quarterly milestones, and 90-day plans offer a stronger alignment with the business cycle of the organization. This simple planning tool, along with the discipline to review it at management meetings and assign accountability for goal achievement, offers a concrete measure of progress. Organizations that integrate 90-day plans into their business processes quickly discover that forward momentum and progress are monitored and shared by all members of the organization.

Give some consideration to what you celebrate in your organization. If you were a visitor, what would these celebrations tell you about what your organization values?

Conclusion

I am often asked whether there is a specific order for navigating the 5C Model and my experience has been that any dimension of the model serves as an entry point for beginning to strengthen change. If you are midway through a change initiative, then I recommend entering at the C of greatest need in your organization. This approach will create the greatest forward momentum for the project.

"There's only one way to come to understand the other person's story, and that's by being curious... Certainty locks us out of their story; curiosity lets us in."

—Douglas Stone, Bruce Patton & Sheila Heen

Chapter 2 • Communication: "Forget the Spin: Say What You Mean to Say"

"Be impeccable with your word. It sounds very simple, but it is very, very powerful."
—Don Miguel Ruiz, *The Four Agreements*

Communication is the open, honest, frequent and strategic sharing of relevant information. Well planned and executed communication can create a sense of community, reassure stakeholders that the leaders of the organization are doing what needs to be done, create space for questions to be answered and ultimately serve as a critical element of a high-performing organization. In today's organizational environments, the credibility of information being shared and the integrity of leaders sharing the information are being questioned. Particularly in a time of uncertainty brought about by change, employees will want to confirm the data for themselves. Business leaders who wish to strengthen trust and ensure that their communications contribute positively to the change effort need excellent communication skills. Bolman and Deal (2008) in their book *Reframing Organizations* offered a four-frame approach for better understanding organizations and how to communicate with individual members and groups. The first frame is the structural frame, which is compared to a factory or machine. People are organized and groups are structured and attuned to task, technology and environment. The second, the human resources frame, is compared to a family, as the focus is on relationships. The leadership challenge in this frame is to align organizational goals with human needs. Third, the symbolic frame

19

includes central concepts such as culture, meaning, metaphor, ritual, ceremony, stories and heroes. The leadership challenge within this frame is fundamentally about creating meaning. Finally, the political frame is about navigating "power, conflict, and organizational politics" (p. 18). The political frame is a unique contribution offered by Bolman and Deal that conveys the importance of developing a variety of interpersonal communication skills. As Bolman and Deal suggested, the political frame is activated whenever there is a scarcity of resources: "The concept of scarce resources suggests that politics will be more salient and intense in difficult times" (p. 196). When navigating the political frame, skills such as influencing, bargaining, negotiation and persuading are helpful. The political frame highlights the reliance on relationships individuals build within organizations.

> *The political frame views authority as only one among many forms of power. It recognizes the importance of individual (and group) needs but emphasizes that scarce resources and incompatible preferences cause needs to collide. The political issue is how competing groups articulate preferences and mobilize power to get what they want. Power, in this view, is not evil.* (Bolman & Deal, 2008, p. 201)

Conger (1998) asserted that both globalization and electronic communication have resulted in a context in which "ideas and people flow more freely than ever around organizations and as decisions get made closer to the markets. These fundamental changes…now firmly part of the economic landscape, essentially come down to this: Work today gets done in an environment where people don't just ask what should I do? but why should I do it?" (pp. 85–86). Conger added that to be able to offer an inspiring response to the why question is to engage in persuasion. Leaders who believe their title is all they need to direct employees to implement change typically discount the idea that the key communication skill is persuasion. However, in the current age of knowledge and collaboration, the leader who can persuade up, across and into the organization, and join with employees in developing shared solutions to problems, can get the job done with involvement and ownership. Collaboration in our global world is extending well beyond the walls of individual organizations. As, Allal-Chéerif (2017) provocatively pointed out when examining the collaborative potential for firms that compete in the same sector, "Their willingness to move forward in the same direction gives them access to unimaginable competitive advantage, makes the future available faster and turns the impossible into possible" (p. 34). In our interconnected world, recognize that without give and take, persuasion is not likely to be effective. In the article titled "The Necessary Art of Persuasion," organizational behavior specialist, Dr. Kathleen Reardon (as cited in Conger, 1998), professor at University of Southern California, offered, "A persuader rarely changes another person's behavior or viewpoint without altering his or her own in the process. To persuade meaningfully, we must not only listen to others but also incorporate their perceptions into our own" (p. 87).

Conger (1998) articulated four essential steps to building capacity in the art of persuasion. The first is establishing credibility through expertise or relationships. The second is identifying, which Conger stressed the importance of when sharing the benefits that exist for the stakeholders. Third, leaders who are effective at persuading others offer evidence. According to Conger (1998),

> *Ordinary evidence, however, won't do. We have found that the most effective persuaders use language in a particular*

way. They supplement numerical data with examples, sto-
ries, metaphors and analogies to make their positions come
alive. That use of language paints a vivid word picture
and, in doing so, lends a compelling and tangible quality to
the persuader's point of view. (p. 92)

In the fourth step, leaders must connect emotionally with followers. Otherwise there is a perceived misalignment of the intended message offered by the leader and what employees take away. Effective communicators have strategies for gaining an appreciation of what the audience is ready to hear. If leaders isolate themselves from their audience, they run a significant risk of being unable to communicate the message that employees most need to hear. Worse still, the message is soundly rejected by the audience because the leader was not perceived as connecting or communicating authentically.

One of the many challenges that leaders face is moving beyond the message they want to communicate. The agenda of communicating "the message" overlooks key elements to effective communication. In their *Harvard Business Review* article, "So You Think You're a Good Listener," Barwise and Meehan (2008) suggested that in "most boss-subordinate relationships, superiors overestimate their openness to receiving difficult messages and simultaneously underestimate the extent to which the power difference discourages subordinates from speaking their minds" (p. 2). Adam Kahane (2010) offered an alternate definition of power for leaders to consider,

Here is how I understand the nature of power and its rela-
tionship to love. Power has two sides, one generative and the
other degenerative. Our power is generative and amplifying
when we realize ourselves while loving and uniting with
others. Our power is degenerative and constraining—reck-

less and abusive, or worse—when we overlook or deny or cut off our love and unity. (pp. 26–27)

I invite you to consider your definition of power and the possibility that exists when as leaders, we operate from Kahane's definition of generative power. Kahane went on to include the pragmatic definition of love articulated by his mentor William O'Brien, the president of Hanover Insurance,

> *In our Western world, the word "love" has deep connotations we do not normally associate with business—romance, for example, or that special feeling among family members or close friends. But I am not talking about these kinds of relationships. By "love," I mean a predisposition toward helping another person to become complete: to develop to their full potential. Love is not something that suddenly strikes us—it is an act of the will. By "an act of will," I mean that you do not have to like someone to love him or her. Love is an intentional disposition toward another person.* (Kahane, 2010, p. 31)

The challenge of communicating authentically during times of change and winning the support of employees begins with the leader. As Secretan (2010) observed,

> *leaders inspire when they approach all activities with a grand aspiration, connecting the dots from the activity, task or communication to a much larger picture. Uninspiring leaders see tasks solely in terms of a metric—Will it make money? Will it help us achieve the budget? Will we get the sale? Will we meet our quality standards? Is it legal? Will it make the analysts happy?* (p. 41)

Morgan (2008) asserted, "Authenticity—including the ability to communicate authentically with others—has become an important leadership attribute" (p. 116). The value of "the second conversation," otherwise known as nonverbal communication, becomes crucial as employees seek alignment between both the nonverbal cues and the message being communicated verbally. Morgan went on to offer leaders four key intentions for creating successful authentic communications. First, be open with your audience. Second, connect with your audience. Third, be passionate about your topic. Fourth, "listen" to your audience.

Leaders who are good communicators are more than good talkers. Embracing communication as a leader during times of change involves challenging the process and boundaries of what can be shared until all the questions we anticipate employees will ask have a response. I find it ironic when I'm in a communications planning session in which energy is directed toward finding a way to avoid bringing up a topic perceived as being "loaded." Also, during times of change, leaders often try to avoid responding to questions that don't have an immediate answer. "I don't know" has somehow become the one thing we don't say. Again, Larkin and Larkin (2006) suggested that imprecise communications are expected at the beginning of a change initiative. Employees do not expect organizational leaders to have all the answers. I encourage leaders to reply by saying, "Great question. I don't have the answer for you at the moment. I commit to having a response to that question by next week." Often what employees are seeking is an acknowledgment that their issue is important. Committing to follow up tells employees that words are followed by actions. The simple act of following through on commitments communicates to employees that they matter in the eyes of the business leader and organization.

To help with planning and communication, start by developing the key messages you need to share.

Table 1. Communication Execution Template

Audience	Message	Materials/ Channels	Responsible	Due Date	Status/ Notes

Finally, as captured in Scanlon's (2008) *Business Week* article "How to Make Meetings Matter," recognize that meetings are a crucial time to communicate. Avoid falling into the trap of conducting meetings on the fly. As Scanlon reported,

> *For most business leaders, planning for a meeting amounts to making a list of agenda items or talking points. But the all-company meeting—or any meeting, for that matter— deserves more attention, even if you're not leading a company through a turnaround. That's because meetings play a powerful role in corporate life. They are both a reflection of an organization's culture and a means of reinforcing that culture. So in big and small and sometimes trivial ways, meetings send employees a message about the company, and if meetings are planned on autopilot, you're probably not sending the right message.* (p. 9)

All forms of communication, including meetings, matter! This is especially true during change because employees are looking for consistent alignment of messages and will dissect anything that doesn't fit with the overall picture being portrayed. From email to conversations with employees to meetings—all these forms of communication matter. In a time of change, properly preparing for meetings, listening and hearing what is concerning employees, and following up on people's concerns communicates to employees that they matter—this is the essence of communication. To close this chapter, I offer self-assessment questions, principles, and action steps to help ensure your communication is relevant, on target and complete. The next chapter explores how confidentiality is key to building trust.

Communication self-assessment questions:

- Who is responsible for leading the communications effort for this change?
- Who is responsible for developing the employee communication strategy?
- Who is responsible for developing the communication strategy for other stakeholders?
- Who is responsible for developing communications?
- Who is responsible for deploying communications?
- What is the status of the communications plan?
- What needs to happen next?
- What concerns do you have?

Communication principles:

- Align the messages and follow-through actions.
- Communicate, communicate, communicate—you can never over-communicate.

Communication action steps:

1. As you wake up every morning, assume that employees want to hear from you and ask yourself this one question: What can I communicate today about this change? Then convey the information through a variety of channels. Repeat daily until the change is deemed complete. This one practice will let employees know that you are aware of their heightened need for information to help alleviate the organizational uncertainty brought on by change initiatives.

2. Develop a communication schedule so that employees know how and when they will receive updates about the change initiative.

3. Determine how managers and supervisors will be updated and briefed to enable them to communicate and address employees' questions.

4. Use the communication execution template included in this chapter to help implement your communications plan.

5. Ask employees how they wish to receive information, and adapt your communication plan accordingly.

6. Maintain an intranet website specific to the change project that captures key updates, records of presentations, updated plans and schedules.

7. Consider "branding" communication related to the change, and follow a regular schedule so employees can anticipate timely receipt of information.

"*Let silence do the heavy lifting*"

—*Susan Scott*

Chapter 3 • Confidentiality: "Be mindful whose secret you are sharing"

"Imagine that every single time others gossip to you, they insert a computer virus into your mind, …then imagine that in an effort to clean up your own confusion and get some relief from the poison, you gossip and spread these viruses to someone else."
— *Don Miguel Ruiz, The Four Agreements*

I am often asked about the rationale for including both Communication and Confidentiality in the 5C Model. Both of these dimensions become possible when each of them is raised within the context of the model. Balancing the need for ongoing communication with the need to respect confidentiality of individual situations is what creates the opportunity for real change to occur. In essence, communication and confidentiality go hand in hand and are built on the foundation of respect.

The first question individual employees ask managers and communicators is, "What does this change mean for me?" If you cannot answer this specific question, prioritize creating a timeline and process for making this information available. It is vital to offer avenues for people to air their concerns, issues, disagreements and insecurities in confidence with a trusted other. This can make all the difference in garnering their support for the change.

Human Dimension of Transition

It is important for organizational leaders to recognize that when people are moving through an externally announced change, there is a significant transition process taking place for people internally. William Bridges offered a powerful model for understanding what occurs for individuals during times of change. Bridges stated,

> *Change is not the same as transition. Change is situational: the new site, the new boss, the new team roles, the new policy. Transition is the internal psychological process people go through to come to terms with the new situation. Change is external, transition is internal.* (2003, p. 3)

Being able to differentiate between change and transition is a valuable concept to help you understand and appreciate the role of honoring the human dimension of change, and the importance of upholding confidentiality during change. Bridges emphasized that transition comprises three distinct phases: endings, the neutral zone and new beginnings.

Endings is a stage that can be characterized by denial, shock, anger and hostility. The challenge of each employee is to accept the reality of the change. In order to honor endings, change leaders are encouraged to find a way to acknowledge the ending. Too often, we plow into change without first honoring and valuing what exists in the organization prior to initiating change. Bridges (2003) offered, "Beginnings depend on endings" (p. 23). Bridges's work helps us to realize the new beginnings we want to see in our organizations require us to create an opportunity to honor what is ending.

What change projects do you have underway in which endings might be honored? When one seeks to create an ending, a symbolic action normally achieves the powerful objective of helping the employees in the organization release "what is" in order to move forward into the second stage of transition. In *The Soul in the Computer*, Barbara Waugh (2001) discussed the ending Hewlett-Packard created when the company made a business decision to separate the computer and instruments sides of the business and make the latter a separate company named Agilent Technologies. Waugh pulled together a team to coordinate a short but powerful transition ceremony to help everyone move into the future.

Waugh worked with a team to set up a tent on the lawn to honor the separation of this community. To this day, that particular moment reminds me of the humanity that is possible when we honor the ending phase of transition. In Waugh's words,

> At the end of the ceremony, we handed each person a beautiful bronze medallion engraved with the globe-in-the-garage logo on both sides. On one side, the text below the garage reads "HP Labs for the World"; on the other it reads "Agilent Labs for the World." Then we ask each person, "Turn your medallion so your new company is facing outward, but know that whichever company you now work for, the other is close to your heart. (p. 142)

I often ask clients, "What small symbolic step to honor endings is possible in your organization?"

I also honor a comment Waugh made about how employees' feelings and thoughts on the one hand have "no place in the normal course of business" yet "left unexpressed, their inner experience is carried forward as a heaviness that slows them down and keeps them from moving into the new with enthusiasm" (p. 141).

I encourage change leaders to ensure that managers, HR practitioners and change practitioners have the opportunity to be sensitized to the experience of employees during periods of significant change. As a result, many clients will offer sessions based on Bridges's (2003) material to both managers and employees. Employees are encouraged to talk to people about their experience during change. We have a responsibility to help our employees build resiliency and provide psychological safety, and that involves accessing coaching, support and safe places to articulate their concerns, without the risk of that information being made public.

A value that came from a team discussion in which I participated many years ago was "honor the absent." It was a powerful moment of learning for me. How often had I found myself saying good things about people that I never communicated directly to them, because I'd said it to someone else. Also, in times of relational challenge, I would find myself talking about someone I was experiencing difficulty with, rather than speaking with that person directly. My lesson learned was to talk *with* people directly, rather than risk talking *about* people in their absence. I recall one participant in a workshop who shared with me that if he found himself in a conversation in which someone was being talked about, he'd suggest that without the person to share their side of the story, perhaps the conversation could be parked to a future time when they were present. Following the completion of the team experience, I committed myself to implementing this value as a practice in my consulting work. In other words, if someone isn't in the room, I don't participate in discussions about my perceptions of that person. Imagine the level of trust in our organizations if this was an agreement that guided our interactions. It has not prevented me from coaching leaders on how to address difficult personnel issues by asking questions and brainstorming courses of action for a particular individual or situation. It has, however, prevented me from adding my perceptions into the discussion. Being mindful to keep my perceptions to myself has helped me to adopt a coach approach and be more client centered. Another action that I have taken to applying, particularly when I'm facilitating leadership development with intact teams, is to introduce "honor the absent" as a potential agreement for the leadership team to consider. I share the above story of my own learning and then invite the team to discuss situations in which an "honor the absent" agreement could operate in service of their work together.

What possibilities exist for you and your organization? What might you add to your change plan to help your management team understand the difference between transition and change? What actions will help ensure that your employees have confidential access to the support they need during periods of turmoil and ambiguity?

Bridges's (2003) second phase is the neutral zone, characterized by resistance to change and by the potential for suffering. Each employee's challenge, then, is to disconnect from the past and overcome resistance to the change. In this middle phase, the importance of balancing the value of communication with the C of Confidentiality is paramount. The experience of suffering and resistance to change requires safe spaces and support so that employees can share their experience, receive support and coaching and move through this period of turmoil. This will enable employees to contribute and add value to the overall change effort. Ignoring employees' needs will yield reduced productivity, a longer period of re-engaging employees, and increased resistance to the overall change initiative.

We know how important it is to communicate with staff. We succeed in changing our environment one conversation at a time. This is particularly true when the conversation is taking place with someone struggling in this neutral zone phase of transition. One of my most powerful forms of honoring others during change is listening and honoring the confidentiality of what is shared. When I lean in and listen in a conversation with someone, I'm amazed at what I learn. Listening to employees experiencing their own individual transitions, and who may be uncomfortable with the ambiguity that is present during change, is a gift.

This gift is particularly valuable during times of transition, and in particular this second phase, listening is key; through listening deeply we enable ourselves to ask significant questions. Brooks and John (2018) stated emphatically, "Most people just don't understand how beneficial good questioning can be. If they did, they would end far fewer sentences with a period - and more with a question mark" (pp. 62-63). Some of my most powerful moments as a leader have been asking a question and watching someone have a deeper conversation with themselves as a result. Often our work as leaders is to help people see possibilities during their time of transition. However, until we can help them identify their issues and concerns, we are limited in our desire to help them shift from viewing change as an either/or event to a place where they can embrace the "and" that change offers. It is during this transitional stage of full uncertainty that confidentiality is vital, and confidentiality is manifest through truly listening. Respecting the confidentiality of these concerns earns leaders tremendous credibility and trust. Until we truly listen, how can we hear the deeper concerns and fears that need to be articulated? Communicating these concerns facilitates a release, which enables a shift from the neutral zone to consider the possibility that the change might offer.

Bridges's (2003) third phase of transition is new beginnings, characterized by exploration, resolution and commitment. The challenge for each employee is to commit to the future and master the new business routines and processes.

I was reminded of this recently when I was teaching graduate leadership students. As part of their course, we analyzed and made recommendations related to a current change. I shared a report drawn from the news and invited the students to complete some small group work related to the loss of 600 Starbucks employee positions and the closure of several locations. I was fascinated that the students had to explore their personal reactions before they could dig into the report I presented to them: "It had better not be my Starbucks." "Where will I get my latte if it's my local Starbucks?" "My family has many memories of Starbucks; I hope it's not our location—I can still remember my daughter in her Christmas dress at that Starbucks."

As Bridges highlighted, there are no new beginnings without endings. Even while discussing a case, I was reminded to let people get oriented to what a change may mean for them. Allowing employees to work through their own transition before moving forward is a critical human lesson. To understand what is taking place, and create space for these conversations to happen. Employees will readily share their concerns and issues. Our role as leaders is to hear those concerns, honor what we hear, support where we can and take action where we see a tangible benefit to the change initiative.

Executives who work for months on a change initiative tell me days after the announcement, "The employees aren't getting it." I remind them they have had months to prepare, and it would be helpful to offer the employees some time to adjust.

Without these very human needs for employees to be heard, to connect and to debate in confidence, dissent will become part of the rumor mill and make it more difficult to gather employee support and commitment. In an organization in which rumors are the only means for people to access information leadership and staff experience significant issues with trust. As Larkin and Larkin (2006) shared in their review of research on rumors, individuals do not intentionally seek to communicate inaccurate information. Organizations have a responsibility to help avoid the communication vacuum created in the absence of frequent, ongoing communication updates (p. 18).

To help employees as they begin to identify what this change means for them, encourage managers and business leaders to communicate early, and to offer updated information on possible outcomes. That way, employees will be able to conduct their own scenario planning for each of the possible outcomes. In confidence, they will be able to approach a trusted other to process their internal experience of transition without starting rumors or falling victim to rumors that have been created in the absence of communication from the organization. This trusted other may be a colleague, a member of the HR department or an internal change management practitioner, supervisor or mentor. Just ensure that transparency exists. This creates the space to discuss the individual impact so that the transition can happen in an environment in which information is readily available and the rumor mill becomes non existent.

On one occasion when I was supporting a significant organizational change project, I found myself following up on every piece of information regarding the status of the project in order to share the most up-to-date information. I wanted to ensure that the information being communicated to the employees was not "stale." It didn't take long for employees to comment on how current the information was. They realized that in some cases, they were the first to receive it publicly. That boosted the momentum in the change effort significantly and allowed individual conversations to take place in an environment of trust and transparency. If we are to help people navigate through Bridge's third stage, it is critical for individuals to learn what this change means to them personally. We can see the importance of accurate, reliable, and timely communication on the engagement of change actors. All of these are cornerstones to building trust. But not all trust is interpersonal. Often it has a larger domain—the organization. And what happens when this organizational trust is threatened?

Organizational Trust

Ryan and Oestreich (1998), in *Driving Fear Out of the Workplace*, introduced me to the concept of placing trust on a continuum, with fear at the opposite end. What a revelation! Organizations that do not actively seek to cultivate trust may be inadvertently cultivating fear.

I recall one client that redesigned its entire management structure to support the change. The client anticipated limited job loss, but not the extent of changes in roles and day-to-day responsibilities. Also, as the organization established each level of the structure, employees needed to apply for the newly named and created positions. In some cases, the successful applicants were former peers of the people who now reported to them. After securing their new positions, they were welcomed to the team and informed that they would now be responsible for the next level of restructuring for their department. For the new members of the management team who were former peers of their direct reports, this was challenging. As part of the individual transition, these newly minted management team members contacted an HR practitioner for a frank discussion on the personal and professional impact this was having on them. They settled into their new positions with the reality of the pending restructuring of their departments weighing heavily upon them. The HR practitioner listened, empathized with their situation and allowed them the space to wrestle with the more challenging aspects of assuming their new positions with confidence. As a result of having a safe person and place to share their concerns, these individuals were able to move forward in their new roles. As you reflect on this, ask yourself who are the trusted others in your organization. What could be done to develop this capacity further across the organization? What would happen if employees considered all managers "trusted others?"

A clear sign of organizational trust is people freely contacting trusted others within the organization for conversations about significant issues they are experiencing. They are not abdicating responsibility for these situations; they are engaging in soliciting alternative points of view and input as they consider how best to move forward. When people feel safe, they access resources familiar with the organizational culture and the inner workings of the organization. Building capacity of leaders, managers, change practitioners and individual contributors to play this role for each other will over time increase organizational trust.

The challenge for organizations and the planning team is to audit their actions on each dimension of the 5C Model in order to avoid emphasizing one dimension at the expense of another. Also, when building specific action steps into the change plan, I encourage change management practitioners to audit each action step against the "intention" it is designed to honor.

Finally, exploring the questions below in relationship to the Confidentiality C can help change agents and leaders alike who wish to enhance employee engagement and strengthen trust building.

Of the 5 Cs, there are two where I encourage leaders to tread carefully: respect for Confidentiality and Cultural Compatibility (the latter will be addressed in the next chapter).

Confidentiality self-assessment questions:

- Does our organization honor confidentiality? In what ways?

- How could honoring confidentiality be strengthened?

- Does our leadership create greater trust in the organization?

- What actions could we take to strengthen trust?

- What actions could we take to reinforce the importance of speaking with, rather than about our colleagues in their absence?

- Does our change initiative allow employees to experience each phase of transition?

Confidentiality principles:

- Allow time for transition to occur.

- Honor the absent.

- Be mindful of when you are selected as a trusted other by an employee and honor the information they share by maintaining its confidentiality.

- Listen when you aren't sure what to say.

- Honor the feelings you hear people expressing, while respecting confidential conversations.

- Identify the fear that may go unexpressed when employees are in transition.

Confidentiality action steps:

1. Have conversations with management about the balance between confidentiality and communication.

2. Provide sessions on Bridges's model of transition to help employees and members of the management team.

3. Ensure that leaders and managers understand that transition does not equal resistance.

4. Consider who the trusted others are in the organization and determine what it would take to build this capacity elsewhere in the organization.

5. Build a transition plan that supports your overall change plan.

6. Identify actions that will create safe spaces in which people can talk and identify safe people for them to talk to as they move through the three phases of transition.

Resources for Strengthening Ourselves and Reframing Resilience

When it comes to living into and leading at our highest and best use of ourselves, one of the precious resources we need to take care of is ourselves. Below are resources to support each of us in strengthening our resilience amidst challenge and opportunity.

Social Resilience Resources

- A non profit dedicated to Gratefulness: https://gratefulness.org/
- Bliss app
- Community: The Structure of Belonging – Peter Block
- The Three Marriages: Reimagining Work, Self and Relationship – David Whyte

Physical Resilience Resources

- Attending to the physical dimensions of health and physical wellbeing
- Healthy eating habits
- Physical care
- Healthy sleep practices

Emotional Resilience Resources

- EQ Fitness Handbook: You In Relationship – 300 Daily Practices to Build EQ Fitness
- Fierce Conversations – Susan Scott
- The Gifts of Imperfection: Let Go of Who You Think You're Supposed to Be and Embrace Who You Are – Brené Brown
- Dare to Lead – Brené Brown
- Kelly McGonigal: How to Make Stress Your Friend https://www.ted.com/talks/
- kelly_mcgonigal_how_to_make_stress_your_friend

Mental Resilience Resources

- Your Mind at Work: SCARF Model – David Rock

- Mindsight: The New Science of Personal Transformation – Daniel Siegel

- Lead through Crisis: What Science says leaders should do with David Rock:
  https://hub.neuroleadership.com/coronavirus-leadership-mar2020-part2?utm_campaign=Coronavirus+Webinar+-+March+2020+Part+2&utm_source=hs_email&utm_medium=email&utm_content=85049451&_hsenc=p2ANqtz-8f25HT-HmgKJ8VhSSHOrSgSJIKhAM6RNZF PvQlSNOOUXQfbk5lyvMZ_Su5URLU3el8jKfk85scYnDNc zL1Ix9Gkivk8w&_hsmi=85049451

Mindfulness

- Jon Kabat Zinn: https://www.mindfulnesscds.com/pages/videos-of-jon-teaching

- BC Association of Living Mindfully: BCALM.ca (resources section is robust)

- Tara Brach: https://www.tarabrach.com/guided-meditations/

- Meditation Apps: HeadSpace, Insight Timer, Calm.com

- See the Internet Resources Section for additional Resilience links

Chapter 4 • Cultural Compatibility: "Together We Can"

"Destroy the culture and you destroy the company."
—*Robert Sutton, Business Week*

The culture of an organization ultimately influences the company's ability to compete successfully in the marketplace. Cultural Compatibility speaks to the importance of the alignment of values, beliefs and principles in an organization. Change generally involves shifting the values in operation within departments, and these are the staff members' coveted ways of being in the world that create a sense of familiarity in the midst of change. In her *Harvard Business Review* article, "The Collaboration Blindspot," Lisa Kwan (2019) pointed out, "groups define and develop their sense of security along three main dimensions: identity, legitimacy, and control. Any leader who wants to encourage effective cross-group collaboration first needs to understand why groups care so much about these dimensions and how they feed into a sense of security" (p. 70). As a result, shifting these values, which is often linked to people's sense of identity, requires persistent effort and ongoing monitoring to avoid the temptation to lapse into the familiar and potentially defensive patterns, such as siloed thinking, protecting information, and avoiding transparent communication.

If you are curious about conducting your own cultural assessment, look around the organizations you visit, as well as your own, and see what people hang on the walls and what the desired takeaway message seems to be.

Begin by looking around at the surroundings in the organization. What organizations want to showcase is hung on the walls in the form of "artifacts." These may be awards, expensive artwork or testimonials from customers; the list is endless. Ask for stories about the founder and other key people, and ask about key moments in the company's history. Stories transmit culture and values in a powerful way. While mission and values statements provide a level of data about what the company says it values, the true test is when these same values are in alignment with the stories that are shared.

The 5C Model does not suggest that if the cultures are different, the change project is in difficulty. It does highlight the importance of actively managing organizational differences within the cultures as part of the overall change plan. The importance of an organization's culture, particularly as a risk factor, cannot be underestimated. Yet far too often, focused efforts to integrate two or more cultures remain the exception rather than the norm. Not actively managing cultural compatibility issues remains a factor in change failures.

So what are the keys to working with cultural compatibility? Simply put, the most critical first step is to acknowledge the culture as it exists today. Often culture is blamed for everything from hierarchy to risk-averse behaviors. I am quick to remind business leaders that before any shifts can take place in the culture, two things must happen.

First, the current culture must be honored for what it has helped the organization to accomplish. Yes, certain aspects of culture may now be serving as a hindrance to the change initiative, and adjustments need to be made. However, until you acknowledge current culture, initiating change will prove challenging. I urge change practitioners to consider that everything in the culture developed at one point in the organization's history as a direct response to an organizational problem or demand. For example, with today's advancements in technology, the monthly report that someone took three weeks to prepare may no longer be relevant, or can be pulled from an alternate source with relative ease. But be cautious of blaming the person who completed it, or of being negative about the reason it was completed. Just remember that such a practice exists because there was a business need for it at an earlier moment in the organization's history.

As part of honoring what is currently in place, I encourage people to be curious about aspects of culture that seem out of place. Second, I encourage everyone involved in the change to recognize one thing: When you talk about culture, you are talking about values. One of the more compelling examples of this type of conversation occurred when I was facilitating a world café (see the Internet Resources section for links to learn more about the world café method and how it can be used). At this event, I was asking for a few comments from the participants regarding the conversation they had been having in their small groups about how they could support each other more fully amidst a change in technology. One participant shared the following: "What I realized in our table conversation is that the system is changing, but the people aren't. We are going to be here to support each other throughout this change." The energy in the room changed after she spoke. It was like everyone in the room exhaled a collective sigh of relief as this insight was shared with the 200 plus people that were present. This moment left a lasting impression on me. In the years since it has prompted me to encourage leaders to also talk about what's not changing, when they talk about change initiatives.

If you have ever participated in a conversation about values, you probably experienced a deeply personal and important dialogue of sharing. Remember, to make shifts in the culture, you are asking people to shift their values. In other words, you are asking for shifts in something that matters deeply. Either they joined the organization because of certain cultural aspects, or they were part of the shared history that fostered these values.

Most people have difficulty articulating the culture of their organization. If this is true for you, talk to a new employee. New employees not fully integrated into the culture can still articulate what they see as "the way things get done around here." They are wonderful cultural anthropologists for your initial assessment of culture. Do you remember starting a new job or joining a new school—in other words, learning about the culture of a not yet familiar organization?

Another powerful opportunity for learning about culture is to pay attention to the stories shared again and again in an organization. As Peter Block (2008) suggested,

> We need to distinguish between the stories that give meaning to our lives and help us find our voice, and those that limit our possibility. The stories that are useful and fulfilling are the ones that are metaphors, signposts, parables and inspiration for the fullest expression of our humanity. They are communal teaching stories. Creation stories, wisdom stories, sometimes personal stories that have a mythic quality, even if they come from the person sitting next to me. (p. 35)

Are the stories shared time and again within your organization tales of creation or those that limit possibility? Consider the potential impact of telling another story and as a result creating the space for a different future for your organization.

The Human Dimension and Culture

Leveraging the value of the human dimension in change and culture is how the possibilities for increasing organizational performance come together.

John Kotter and James Heskett, both professors at the Harvard Business School,

> studied the impact of organizational culture on long-term economic performance (Kotter and Heskett 1992). They found that organizations significantly outperformed others when they were committed to and consistently reinforced a philosophy focused on two elements:
>
> 1. the needs and interests of employees, as well as those of customers and stockholders
>
> 2. development and support of effective leadership among all levels of management, with important leadership characteristics that include openness, a strong power base, seeing the need for change, articulating the vision and strategy, and motivating large groups of people to make things happen. (Kotter & Heskett, as cited in Ryan & Oestreich, 1998, p. 108)

In their article "Strengthening Human Value in Organizational Cultures," Stallard and Pankau (2008) identified six human psychological needs as part of their research in organizations: respect, recognition, belonging, autonomy, personal growth and meaning (p. 20). Stallard and Pankau also asserted, "Leaders are discovering the powerful effect of fostering a culture that values people and connects leaders, employees and customers" (p. 19). So, as we seek to assess the cultural compatibility within our organizations, one of the questions we can audit ourselves against is, to what extent are we providing workplaces that meet these six psychological needs? The request being made in cultural compatibility is one of belonging. In his book *Community: The Structure of Belonging*, Peter Block (2008) had this to say: "Community offers the promise of belonging and calls for us to acknowledge our interdependence. To belong is to act as an investor, owner and creator of this place" (p. 3). Block went on to assert,

> *The small group is the unit of transformation. It is in the structure of how small groups gather that an alternative future will be created… Belonging can occur through our membership in large groups, but this form of belonging reduces the power of citizens. Instead of surrendering our identity for the sake of belonging, we find in the small group a place that can value our uniqueness.* (p. 31)

More and more, in my practice, I am noticing an opportunity for organizations to cultivate a sense of belonging for employees. This intentional work is yielding a stronger sense of relational connectedness, which offers several other positive impacts. It can start with something as simple as goals. As Danella Meadows (2008) articulated, "Harmonization of goals in a system is not always possible, but it's an option worth looking for. It can be found only by letting go of more narrow goals and considering the long-term welfare of the entire system" (pp. 115–116). And harmonizing goals is one possible starting point on this organizational journey.

Most individuals in organizations have an individual identity as they enter organizations, and if they experience a sense of belonging and a commitment to purpose in these organizations, a sense of "we" evolves over time. However, I am struck by a rare situation that I have observed that doesn't often occur, and that is the very powerful shift to "us." So, the journey is one of me, to we, to us. Me to we happens in many organizations. We to us is a much rarer occurrence. Perhaps the work occurring at Google as reported by Duhigg (2016) offers some guideposts to the potential for becoming an "us" in our organizations over time. Too often, I believe our relationship and identity to our department limits the possibility of moving beyond we to truly become us. If you reflect on your own organization and see a strong identity to a department, project team, or unit, you are seeing we in action. At the level of we, the organization may still experience silos, departmental protection strategies, politicking, and ultimately a we-versus-they mentality within the organization. The shift to us occurs in those rare instances when the sense of belonging is to the organization, and the vision of what the organization can be becomes the identifier for the organizational members. Essentially, the vision and purpose of the organization serves as the foundation for collaboration and decision making. In recent years, I know that I have seeded the possibility of this journey to us each time I, as a university instructor welcome a new cohort of graduate learners to their residency intensive I offer the notion of "us" as an intentional opportunity to gain the experience of what it feels like to cultivate an "us" that they can then take back to their organizations. In this case, the sense of belonging and support can cultivate collaboration that transcends teamwork and the individual pursuit of completion of the graduate program to include a community of practice and relationships that are relied on well into the future. My hope is the working professionals who pursue graduate learning will steward this possibility, because the commitment to cultivating us is a key to successfully operating in complex, adaptive environments.

Figure 2. Me, We, and Us

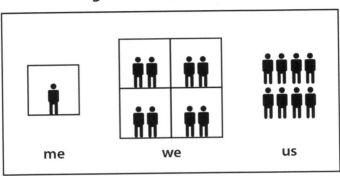

me   we   us

In a 2008 article, "Employee Motivation: A Powerful New Model," Nohria, Groysberg, and Lee summarized four basic emotional needs initially set out in the work of Lawrence and Nohria. These are the drives to (a) acquire—obtain scarce goods, including intangibles such as social status, (b) bond—form connections with individuals and groups, (c) comprehend—satisfy our curiosity and master the world around us and (d) defend—protect against external threats and promote justice (Nohria et al., 2008, p. 80). In their article these authors speak directly to the importance of culture when they state, "The most effective way to fulfill the drive to bond—to engender a strong sense of camaraderie— is to create a culture that promotes teamwork, collaboration, openness and friendship" (Nohria et al., 2008, p. 82). As we seek to involve our employees in change initiatives that include the assessment and management of cultural compatibility, we have plenty of evidence to suggest that offering employees ways to meet these needs and drives will strengthen our overall organizational performance. As Secretan (2010) noted,

> It is not a coincidence that Google, Southwest Airlines, Amazon and Starbucks (even though their short-term fortunes may fluctuate) receive ten times as many applications as they have available job opportunities, while "old-story" organizations constantly struggle to recruit replacements for those fleeing from their uninspiring environments. (p. 132)

Ronald Short has an unpublishd manuscript that articulates the theory of two organizations. Short referred to Organization 1 as technical systems and Organization 2 as living, relational systems to explain the presence of the dual organization in operation. To use his terminology, Organization 1 is the technical system where staff talk about "it": the widget that needs to be made, the markets that need to be penetrated, the shareholder value that needs to be increased, and the change that needs to be managed. This is the organization we can measure. It's quantitative, focused on what organizational members can see. We know this organization well. We talk about "it" a lot (R. Short, personal communication, February 7, 2010). In Learning in Relationship, Short (1998) described conversations about "it" as an example of a non-learning pattern,

> It can be anything—a situation, event, object, another person, beliefs... whatever... You don't learn from your interactions when you talk only about it or an object and do not disclose here-and-now why you are talking about it, and how you feel talking about it, and how you feel talking with the other person about it. (pp. 103–104)

Organization 2 is the living, relational system or "now" organization. Here, we are always dealing with the present, the now. It's a qualitative organization. It's what staff believe. It's the inside-out organization. Both levels operate in all organizations.

If you are having difficulty experiencing these parallel organizations in operation, take a few moments and complete this brief exercise. First, take out a sheet of paper and make a list of what is occupying you right now. Identify three or more priorities you are working on. Now, set the list aside. Take a few moments. Place your feet on the floor, close your eyes and sit quietly. Take three deep breaths. In and out. As you exhale, breathe out what's occupying your mind. As you inhale, breathe in the life-giving oxygen of this room, now. In and out. Okay, open your eyes. Welcome to the present moment or NOW, also known as Organization 2. Do you feel different now than you did before? Before was Organization 1, the technical system; now is Organization 2, the living relational system. Be here NOW and you are living in Organization 2. It's that simple and that hard. The exercise highlights the importance of being present in our organization to what is happening now. Ronald Short challenges us to develop the capacity for describing our present moment experience, because what we have is this moment. Too often our lives are preoccupied with what happened in the past or will happen in the future at the expense of what is happening right now.

As you return to the list you wrote before the breathing exercise, you may notice that it speaks to what needs to be done, which is indicative of the Organization 1 or technical system. Also, is the list indicative of a past or future focus? What could you add to it to remind you of the importance of this moment or Organization 2? The power to effect change in "how we do things around here" is in the present moment, and it is in our power to describe our experience in that moment. This present moment awareness is important. Becoming aware of Organization 2 is critical to our awareness of culture and our capacity to make shifts in service of the culture and the organization.

One of the more memorable lessons Ron Short taught me came at the end of a four-day workshop. As the participants had a final after-workshop lunch, a participant noticed the time and commented on his need to get to the airport so as not to miss his flight. Ron looked at him and said, "It just happened." I looked around to see "what" might have just happened, not realizing that Ron was pointing out an internal shift that had taken place for this participant. Ron explained that the consequence of thinking about missing the flight had prompted increased anxiety for the individual. Anxiety can alert us to the fact that we are no longer in the present moment. Anxiety robs us of our present moment experience and we experience it only as we focus on past events that caused us worry and future events that may cause us worry. A past or future focus is one way to ensure we are anywhere but in our present moment. As we navigate change, one of the most powerful tools available to us as change practitioners is to be present to our moment-by-moment experience, or in Ron Short's words, present in Organization 2 or the NOW organization.

When assessing cultural compatibility, focus on working in both the technical and living levels of the organization. If we only talk about "it," we never talk about the living organization, which is what matters most to people. It's not possible to be present in the now if we are in the past or future.

Who Owns the Culture?

This question generally sparks spirited conversations at client sites. I recall attending a plant quarterly meeting while the new CEO was visiting the branch. He led the meeting in an open Q&A format after sharing the quarterly results. When asked about his experience of the company culture, he proceeded to share his findings. Earlier, as he had toured various company sites, employees had told him which aspects of culture they were proud of and how much ownership they took in their site. In the meeting, he observed that employees appeared to be under the impression they "owned" the culture.

"Wrong answer. I own the culture," he told the assembled group. It was as if a buzzer had sounded in the room. He went on to describe the various organizational "levers" he was implementing to realign the culture. Certainly, several levers exist within organizational culture that can incentivize desired behaviors. However, I argue that ownership of the culture does not rest with the CEO exclusively.

To understand more fully who owns the culture, let's look briefly at a critical moment in the history of a new airline in the U.S., Southwest Airlines. The video *Southwest Airlines Company Culture: Out of the Ordinary* shares the following story. When Southwest began operations, initial planning included a schedule for four planes. However, the firm needed to sell one plane for necessary cash. Schedules had been published and customers had purchased fares. The norm in the industry at the time was 90 minutes or more to "turn" a plane. Preparing a plane for the next flight included cleaning, unloading baggage, bringing on new crew, reloading baggage, refueling and completing the inspections. The leadership team solicited employee involvement in what it would take to create a 20-minute "turn." Southwest had realized an important potential point of leverage for success: Planes made more money when they were in the air, and activities that resulted in less time on the ground were crucial to success. In this significantly unionized environment, the culture of working together to achieve seemingly difficult if not impossible goals supported the success of Southwest Airlines. Within the airline industry, Southwest Airlines, over one 5-year period, experienced the best on-time performance and the fewest complaints for lost baggage.

So, who owns the culture becomes a question worth considering, and Ron Short (1998) offered a compelling perspective in *Learning in Relationship:*

> *Your organization is made up of your relationships and the very specific interactions you have with specific individuals, in specific contexts, over specific issues. You and those with whom you interact define what your organization is—the limits of what you can do and become. These interactions are the "genetic code" for your organization, and they contain the information you need to learn… Without you, your organization doesn't exist. Any effort to change your organization has to begin with you and your specific interactions with specific individuals. Why is this realization so important? Because I have seen the opposite assumption play out time and time again. It is far more typical for individuals in an organization or a team to want others to change before they do.* (p. 17)

It's often tempting to cite the problem as being external to us. However, when we are working with organizational culture, it starts and ends with us. How we show up in our organizations, the conversations we have, the issues that prompt our passion and the perpetual conflicts we can't seem to shake, all contribute to defining the culture we experience. As we begin to consider this perspective, Gervase Bushe (2001), a proponent of moving beyond problems and deficit-based approaches to looking at culture, pointed out,

> *When all we do in our organizational life is go from one crisis to the next, one problem to another, work becomes drudgery, or worse, paralyzing. The only time action is mobilized is when you have a serious problem. You can't create a climate of continuous learning and improvement in a problem-oriented culture. Such cultures develop a "don't fix it unless it's broken" map, for good reason: They have so many already broken things to fix.* (p. 158)

As we begin to identify specific approaches for working with culture, let's ask ourselves the question Barry Johnson (1996) is so famous for asking: "Is this a problem to solve or a polarity to manage?" As we move into the next section, consider that cultural differences may indicate creative tensions (Senge, 2006) that need to be actively managed, as opposed to eliminated or suppressed because they are no longer serving the organization. As I reflect on one of the current impacts on organizational culture, I consider the simultaneous presence of three or more generations in our organizations. With a minimum of three generations represented, we are experiencing added complexity, varying expectations, diverse values, and different career priorities. All of these differences are amplified amidst the uncertainty brought forward by change. As a result, cultivating a sense of shared belonging, values, and purpose despite our differences becomes a powerful culture lever to support positive change outcomes.

Polarity Management and Culture

In his book *Polarity Management: Identifying and Managing Unsolvable Problems,* Barry Johnson (1996) offered a powerful tool for holding the container of culture. His work applies to several organizational issues. It offers a strategic opportunity for individuals wishing to maintain seemingly different aspects of organizational culture. I recall in my work with a telecommunications company the very different subcultures that existed across the organization, and how these differences supported the overall organization more fully. For example, a research and development department exploring new products and markets would function differently than a manufacturing department producing large quantities each week that are of consistent quality. Depending on the environment, expectations that all members of the organization have the same set of values in operation may or may not be in the best interests of the organization.

According to Johnson (1996), two questions determine whether you have a problem to solve or a polarity to manage: "Is the difficulty ongoing?" and "Are there two poles which are interdependent?" (p. 82). First determine whether the difficulty is ongoing. Typically a problem has a solution that can be implemented over time. In the case of a polarity, Johnson (1996) said,

> Polarities to manage are sets of opposites which can't function well independently. Because the two sides of a polarity are interdependent, you cannot choose one as a "solution" and neglect the other. The objective of the Polarity Management™ perspective is to get the best of both opposites while avoiding the limits of each. (p. xviii)

Here is an example of interdependent opposites in action. Once when I was talking with a leadership team, I began to see how their urgent requirements drove their schedules. Unfortunately, important high priority items never seemed to get addressed. Completing the urgent work within an impossible deadline generated a sense of achievement. However, important tasks weren't getting tackled. As a result, employees were frustrated with management, which seemed to go from crisis to crisis without dealing with practical issues that would give employees a greater sense of stability. As I described this polarity, the management team also began to see how they consistently shifted from one urgent deadline to the next. We identified strategies for dealing with some of the important issues. Once the leadership team recognized that these were two interdependent opposites that needed to be managed over time, rather than focusing on one of the opposites at the expense of the other, the leadership team could address both the urgent and important priorities in their work.

In *Polarity Management*, Johnson (1996) identified a polarity map that articulates the upsides of each interdependent opposite. Underneath each upside is the downside of focusing only on the one upside. If I were using the example above, and I focused only on the urgent items in my priority list, what unfortunate consequences might begin to arise over time? What impact might an organization experience if only urgent items are addressed? The goal here is to recognize that each upside has a downside and that if you are dealing with interdependent opposites, you can focus only on one of the opposites for so long before the downside emerges and you find yourself compelled to shift. In my example of the urgent-important polarity, how long would it take before important items become crises because they weren't addressed in a timely manner?

Laura Harvell, a consultant, uses the polarity management approach when working with clients experiencing shifts in culture. After offering some context-setting material by discussing the principles of William Bridges (2003) which I presented in Chapter 3, she begins by having people break into four groups. Each group rotates through the following four tasks:

1. What are the best aspects of your organization's past and present culture that you would like to take forward (things you want to retain from the past)?

2. What aspects of your organization's past and present culture do you want to leave behind? What are the fears and concerns of focusing only on the past or present?

3. What cultural attributes do you want in your organization in the future that you don't currently have?

4. What are your concerns or fears of the future direction?

In debriefing the output of these tasks, each of the four tasks aligns with an aspect of the values of the desired culture. Task 1 explores pride: What is it that people take pride in within their organization? Task 2 explores complaints, recognizing that there are generally aspects of culture that no longer work well. Task 3 invites participants to focus on vision, the idea that we can co-create something together. Finally, Task 4 creates space for a conversation on what we wish to avoid, by exploring the deeper fears and concerns about the future direction of the combined organization. The debrief allows for holding the differences that inevitably show up. Participants also have the opportunity to consider new possibilities. Hopefully participants will prioritize and agree on desired culture attributes.

Johnson's (1996) model and work offer us a powerful tool for recognizing and affirming the values people hold dear in our organizational cultures. It enables us to explore how we affirm and recognize values that at the outset might appear mutually exclusive. For more information on polarity management, see the References and Internet Resources sections. As Peter Koestenbaum (2003) so aptly articulated in *The Many Facets of Leadership*, "Forcing a choice in a polarity is to try clapping with one hand" (p. 152). Polarity management is one of many tools that help us hold the container of differences in our organizations in a way that honors the differences rather than making one right or better than the other.

Cultural Compatibility self-assessment questions:

- Do we have cultural compatibility?

- Are there shifts that we wish to make in the culture?

- What behaviors can the leadership team begin to model to align the message with the actions of the organization?

- What sensitive cultural issues do we expect to encounter as part of the change initiative?

Cultural Compatibility principles:

- Honor the culture that is already in place. This culture evolved to respond to valid business challenges that may be less relevant today.

- Shifts in culture occur and they must be managed with care as they have a direct relationship to what people value.

- Employee involvement in the shifts will accelerate the pace of culture change.

Cultural Compatibility action steps:

1. Explore polarity management as a tool for thinking about culture.

2. Pay attention to the messages offered by the stories that are told and retold, as they provide critical insights about what the people in the organization value.

3. Notice what artifacts communicate to you about what the organization values.

4. What the organization celebrates and acknowledges also offers insight about what is valued.

"A shared vision is...a force in people's hearts, a force of impressive power. It may be inspired by an idea, but once it goes further—if it is compelling enough to acquire the support of more than one person—then it is no longer an abstraction. It is palpable."

—Peter Senge

Chapter 5 • Courtship: "Why?"

"Great leadership is about human experiences, not processes. Leadership is not a formula or a program; it is a human activity that comes from the heart and considers the hearts of others."
—Lance Secretan, *Inspirational Leadership*

Courtship is the "why" of this change initiative—the vision, strategy and the reason. Courtship invites stakeholders to realize the desired future that successful change will create. Beckhard and Harris (1987) first introduced us to this concept when they presented a change process that asked us to describe our present state, and then describe our desired future state. The space between these two states was known as the transition state, intended to define what it would take to accomplish the shift to the desired future. To leverage courtship, one must fully describe the desired future state.

Clients often ask me if courtship is really necessary once the decision has been made to proceed with the change initiative. My response is, it is even more important. It highlights the significance of operating with a "spirit of invitation" throughout the change. Courtship emphasizes the value of encouraging involvement of stakeholders to create a sense of ownership for the change. For organizational change to be successful, ownership has to be distributed among numerous stakeholders and it is not enough to demand that it happen. Too often, leaders who see the change as necessary but haven't yet persuaded the employees of such will say, "It's their job to make it happen."

But in today's marketplace, I say it's their *choice*, not their job, to make it happen, and it's the task of leadership to set up the conditions for employees to want to make it happen. This results in a significant shift for leaders being called on to build capacity in several different domains. Suddenly, the gap between an unsuccessful and successful change initiative widens. I believe leadership is key to narrowing that gap.

Courtship is a fairly provocative term to use in conjunction with change. Often it brings up images more suited to a personal life than business situation. However, if we think back to organizational courtship, especially executive recruiting, the parallels begin to surface. Courtship shows up all the time at work. It's about reminding executives and change management practitioners to sell change and to avoid telling people to change, because telling doesn't generally generate the desired results.

What are the keys to creating a positive organizational courtship for successful change? There are three levers that strengthen courtship. First is leadership. Ultimately, successful change is about relationships and the need to maintain and strengthen them throughout the process. Second is emotional intelligence: the capacity for self-reflection, self-regulation, and empathy. This allows for harvesting key learning moments in the change initiative to achieve success. The leadership discipline of actively engaging in reflective practice to support identification of next actions is well documented (Page & Margolis, 2017; Raelin, 2018; Senge 2006). Third, organizational courtship must have a clear, decisive, strategic purpose and direction. From the outset, organizational stakeholders, especially employees, need to know why they are being asked to enter a period of uncertainty and ambiguity. Stakeholders will wonder, "Why are we doing this now?" Without a clearly articulated answer to that question, employees remain hesitant, uncommitted, and quite likely resistant. Change is hard enough without employees' ambivalence as an obstacle.

What happened to the age-old mantra that suggests people should leave their heart at the door when they enter the workplace? No longer is this the case. Research has demonstrated the value of heart in the workplace, especially if we wish to leverage creativity and innovation. As Barsh, Capozzi and Davidson (2008) asserted,

> *Innovation is inherently associated with change and takes attention and resources away from efforts to achieve short-term performance goals. More than initiatives for any other purpose, innovation may therefore require leaders to encourage employees in order to win over their hearts and minds.* (p. 39)

As organizations continue to evolve and today's workplaces experience a diversity of culture and generations, work engagement needs have shifted dramatically. Employees are no longer committed to organizations. They are committed to purpose, to being part of something bigger than themselves, to the possibility of work that will make a difference. If leaders can't or won't inspire this quest to create legacy, then the unintended consequence is a lack of discretionary effort.

To support your leadership efforts and inspire employees to invest their best efforts, I recommend you familiarize yourself with the work of Gervase Bushe. In his book *Clear Leadership*, Bushe (2001) invited leaders to develop an appreciative mindset. Specifically, he asked, "What happens when we let go of a deficit mind-set and develop an appreciative mind-set?"

The appreciative mind-set chooses to pay attention to things it can value, care about, be happy with and want more of… This means, first of all, being clear about what you want more of… Appreciative processes are used to amplify things—to create inter-subjective reality by increasing the amount or frequency of something you want more of… Second, for it to be a truly appreciative mind-set, you need to be calling to something that touches people's imagination, their aspirations and spirit… Opportunities to excel, make a difference, grow and develop, achieve our potential, be the best, live in community, make a better world, fulfill our dreams, gain new hope, surpass expectations, be a winner, enable the children, ennoble our spirit, be a part of a dynamic and caring team, be in real partnership with others, make a valued contribution—these are the kinds of things that an appreciative self pays attention to. (pp. 164–165)

Leaders are the individuals that employees will follow in times of change. When I ask employees what led to their commitment to the change, it starts with the name of someone in the organization whom the employee respects—the leader. In *The Leadership Challenge,* Kouzes and Posner (2007) help leaders who wish to be this person for their employees. Their work documents the results of a research project that began more than 30 years ago as Kouzes and Posner sought to learn "what people did when they were at their 'personal best' in leading others" (p. xiii). The findings offer significant guidance and practical tools to leaders who wish to expand both their capacity to lead and their effectiveness as leaders. Specifically, Kouzes and Posner (2007) identified five leadership practices: "model the way, inspire a shared vision, challenge the process, enable others to act and encourage the heart" (p. 26). Heifetz and Linksy (2002), in *Leadership on the Line*, spoke about the role of the sacred heart in leadership,

> *A sacred heart is an antidote to one of the most common and destructive challenges of modern life: numbing oneself. Leading with an open heart helps you stay alive in your soul. It enables you to feel faithful to whatever is true, including doubt, without fleeing, acting out or reaching for a quick fix. Moreover, the power of a sacred heart helps you to mobilize others to do the same—to face challenges that demand courage, and to endure the pains of change without deceiving themselves or running away.* (p. 230)

Kotter and Cohen (2002), in *The Heart of Change* (2002), emphasized the importance of leading with heart: "People change what they do less because they are given analysis that shifts their thinking than because they are shown a truth that influences their feelings" (p. 1).

These researchers and authors, all significant contributors to the field of leadership, asserted that heart and leadership are interdependent. Leaders inspire by what they say, how they show up in their organizations and the behaviors they exhibit every day. Organizations wishing to fully embrace the organizational courtship dimension should pay attention to who is leading the change initiative. Identify individuals with credibility and ensure that they receive the support needed to continue expanding their leadership capacity. Only then will the organization experience the benefits of forward momentum, employee ownership and greater stakeholder collaboration.

We are all leaders, whether on the soccer field, in our families, in our volunteer pursuits or in our organizations. Moments of doubt are part of leadership—moments when the path is not clear and organizational leadership is desperately needed. When I work with leaders, my main interest is in what happens when things aren't going well, when the organization is in crisis or turmoil. Time and again I've observed that leaders with self-awareness, self-regulation and empathy are able to renew, rejuvenate and restore both the organization and its employees. In the next section we will further explore emotional intelligence.

Emotional Intelligence and Leadership

In the *Harvard Business Review* article "Leading by Feel," Daniel Goleman (2004) suggested the following,

> *You can be a successful leader without much emotional intelligence if you're extremely lucky and you've got everything else going for you: booming markets, bumbling competitors and clueless higher-ups. If you're incredibly smart, you can cover for an absence of emotional intelligence until things get tough for the business. But at that point, you won't have built up the social capital needed to pull the best out of people under tremendous pressure.* (p. 28)

As part of my workshops on emotional intelligence, I ask attending business professionals, MBA learners, and undergraduates to identify a learning objective for the topic. They often say they want to understand what emotional intelligence is and whether or not people have the capacity to develop emotional intelligence. Some also wonder what role emotional intelligence plays in leadership.

Contrary to what popular business literature has said, it was Salovey and Mayer (1990) who originally defined the term,

Emotional intelligence [is] a set of skills hypothesized to contribute to the accurate appraisal and expression of emotion in oneself and in others, the effective regulation of emotion in self and others, and the use of feelings to motivate, plan and achieve in one's life. (p. 185)

In the past 30 years, several authors have furthered Salovey and Mayer's work. *Learning in Action Technologies* in particular offers business leaders practical guidance through their "EQ in Action Profile," which measures individuals and teams on three capacities defined in *EQ Fitness Handbook*. First, self-reflection involves "the ability to observe our thoughts, feelings and behavior in the moment as we participate in life" (Johnson, 2010, pp. 10–11). In the 2004 article "Leading by Feel," former Medtronic CEO William George spoke about the importance of finding one's voice: "Authentic leadership begins with self-awareness, or knowing yourself deeply. Self-awareness is not a trait you are born with but a capacity you develop throughout your lifetime" (p. 35).

The second capacity is empathy, which Johnson (2010) defined as "the capacity to feel connected with another person and experience their pain or joy. It is the ability to walk in another's shoes and to understand what a given situation must feel like from their perspective" (p. 11).

Finally, the third capacity is self-regulation or ability "to experience the distress and pain that are natural parts of life and to manage them in ways that help us re-establish our equilibrium or balance without requiring others to change" (Johnson, 2010, p. 11).

Organizations wishing to fully leverage organizational courtship must actively develop the emotional intelligence of leaders who are leading the change initiative. Based on her review of the literature, Kerry Webb (2009) said, "A considerable body of research now suggests that the key to success lies in a person's ability to perceive, identify and manage emotion" (p. 36). Webb summarized the work of researcher Fabio Sala, who offered a four-phase process for developing emotional intelligence in the workplace: preparation, training, transfer and maintenance and evaluation (p. 38). For leaders seeking to navigate change successfully, emotional intelligence is key for development and capacity building. Employees and their organizations are well served by leaders who share themselves and their humanity authentically with employees.

Can individuals develop emotional intelligence? Several researchers and authors in the field respond with a resounding yes, adding that we can continue to develop it as we age. As Johnson (2010) offered,

> *We have increasing evidence that emotions are the ultimate driver of everything we do and that by becoming conscious of those emotions, we can actually shape how our brains respond to them. In other words, being aware in the moment of our emotional experience can help us make effective and satisfying choices about our actions and attitudes.* (p. 9)

Leaders open to developing any of the three capacities will find *EQ Fitness Handbook* a rich resource. It is available electronically, via Amazon. Further inspiration for cultivating a leadership practice that cultivates opportunities for us to increase our self-awareness comes from the late Ojibway elder, Richard Wagamese (2016),

> *My spiritual father once told me, "Nothing in the universe ever grew from the outside in." I like that. It keeps me grounded. It reminds me to be less concerned with outside answers and more focused on the questions inside. It's the quest for those answers that will lead me to the highest possible version of myself.* (Wagamese, 2016, p. 23).

As leaders, asking questions creates the reflective space for us to explore the answers so that when interacting with employees, leaders are well positioned to offer much needed perspective.

Organizational courtship is complete when we can clearly communicate the "why" of the change initiative. For this to happen, leaders must clarify the strategy and organizational purpose of the change initiative.

Clarifying Strategy

As noted earlier, being able to describe the "desired state" at the beginning of a change is key to fully leveraging the C of Courtship. The challenge is clarifying strategy. If, as a leader in your organization, you are sitting at the table during strategy development, congratulations. Your task will be much easier. However, not all leaders work at corporate headquarters, nor are they invited to help develop and articulate strategy. Instead, they find themselves interpreting it for employees within their division. This is a challenge for those who wish to actively engage employees in the dialogue. Such leaders need to give employees enough clarity about strategy to respond to the question, "Why are we engaging in this change initiative now?" Even when the strategy has been developed elsewhere, the leadership challenge remains the same. For organizational courtship to be successful and for cultivation of employee involvement and ownership to take place, leaders have to translate the strategy and help employees understand its immediate relevance to their situation.

How does this change fit within the long-term business strategy of the organization? As Hamel and Prahalad (as cited in Senge, 2006) noted, "Although strategic planning is billed as a way of becoming more future oriented, most managers, when pressed, will admit that their strategic plans reveal more about today's problems than tomorrow's opportunities" (p. 196).

What is strategy? According to DeKluyver and Pearce (2003) in *Strategy: A View from the Top,*

> *Strategy should focus on creating value—for shareholders, partners, suppliers, employees and the community—by satisfying the needs and wants of customers better than anyone else... What is valuable today, might not be valuable tomorrow. The moral of this story is simple but powerful: The value of a particular product or service offering, unless constantly maintained, nourished and improved, erodes with time.* (p. 3)

In *Integrated Strategic Change,* Worley, Hitchin and Ross (1996) asserted,

> *The only truly sustainable competitive advantage is the capability to make the transition from one set of strategies, structures and processes that exploit an old advantage to another strategic orientation that exploits a new advantage—in short, the capability to design and implement strategic change.* (p. 7)

Important questions to consider prior to engaging employees in dialogue about the change initiative include:

- What is the business case for the change?

- At what level in the organization are people going to be affected by the change?

- As the leader, what is your personal commitment to the change?

- How does this change fit with the long term business strategy?

Courtship means providing the answers to these questions when employees ask. Organizational courtship involves minimizing ambiguity. We owe ourselves and our employees nothing less than clarity when we can provide it. Preparing to achieve clarity is a key leadership challenge. It also communicates to stakeholders that we are seeking their help and involvement because it will make a difference in the success of the overall change effort. If you were an employee asked to be involved in a change initiative, wouldn't you want to know that your involvement mattered? And that the goal was clearly articulated at the outset so you knew what you were being asked to accomplish?

As Ronald Heifetz (2004) summarized in the *Harvard Business Review* article, "Leading by Feel":

> *Leadership couples emotional intelligence with the courage to raise the tough questions, challenge people's assumptions about strategy and operations—and risk losing their goodwill. It demands a commitment to serving others; skill at diagnostic, strategic and tactical reasoning; the guts to get beneath the surface of tough realities and the heart to take heat and grief.* (p. 37)

Courtship self-assessment questions:

- Why are we doing this change now?

- How does this change align with our strategy? Our purpose?

- Who is being tasked with leading this change initiative?

- What further support does the change leader require?

Courtship principles:

- Inspire commitment and ownership to the change.

- Ensure that each conversation with employees about the change is leveraged to hear and address concerns.

- Sell, don't tell.

Courtship action steps:

1. Develop a clear and concise statement of alignment with the strategy of the organization.

2. Continually revisit the purpose for the change.

3. Identify the benefits the employees will experience along with the organizational benefits.

4. Be mindful of leader selection for the change.

5. Focus on developing an appreciative mindset.

Chapter 6 • Completion: "We're Done!"

"Ceremonies, celebrations and rituals are not about the event. They're about touching the hearts and souls of every employee."
—*Victoria Sandvig (as cited in Kouzes & Posner, 2003)*

Completion is the acknowledgment of achieving ongoing milestones and intentional closure for the change project. Encourage change management teams to plan ahead for completion. Begin with the end in mind. For example, identify what the measures of success are to allow change management teams to track and monitor progress toward completion throughout the project. Some teams hold onto key artifacts to use as part of a completion celebration. If you know at the outset what completion will look like, you'll document with intention the important emails, photos, events and milestones so that they can become part of the completion celebration. Too often, I have sat in meetings that never clearly defined the notion of completion. As a result, employees participate in a project that never seems to end. As Lance Secretan (2010) said,

> We are a species that seeks completion and order. Loose ends and untidiness frustrate; conclusions and closure offer a sense of satisfaction and tidiness—an inner pleasure that flows from the completion of tasks, projects or missions. (p. 22)

As we explore the possibilities of creating and managing completion in our organizations, certain tools help facilitate the process. First, clearly articulate what completion looks like by identifying outcomes and measures. Second, create milestones that allow for mini-celebrations at midpoints of success. Third, identify some opportunities for mobilizing momentum and honoring progress. Finally, seek to celebrate the achievement that follows completion. Completion, properly defined at the beginning of the project, creates wonderful opportunities for mobilizing employees throughout the change project.

Creating Milestones

Identifying and monitoring project milestones creates forward momentum for employees, senior management and other stakeholders. The challenge is to create milestones sufficiently detailed that everyone can checkmark them on completion. Completion identifies the importance of making the time to define and revisit milestones.

Great milestones meet a few identifying characteristics. First, they are adequately described so that all stakeholders can agree when one has been achieved. Initially, this may be difficult, but by revisiting the milestones periodically as more detail becomes available, all stakeholders will clearly understand what milestone achievement means. I once worked on a project with a completion milestone of a new system "going live." Unfortunately, "go live" means different things to different people. It could include:

- The system was distributed on the servers and available for users to enter

- Users were using the system

- People could extract useful data or reports from the system

- Users were trained and using the system appropriately

- Parallel systems were no longer in use

- The system was meeting requirements and performing tasks it was designed to perform with few or no errors.

Or, all of these characteristics could have been included to form the criteria for completion. The lesson? Ensure that you define the acceptable error rate as part of defining that the system is meeting requirements.

Too often, the detail is missing and the project manager says, "We aren't done because X hasn't happened yet and the leadership team is being pressured to remove the obstacles." How much simpler life would be if the criteria were described in detail at the beginning of a project and each milestone had specific data associated with it. All stakeholders could then agree as each criterion was met.

Mobilizing Forward Momentum

The key to navigating change successfully is being able to actively contribute to factors mobilizing forward momentum. One way to help employees see progress is to break down the overall project into achievable chunks. Once you've established project milestones, each group contributing to the change project needs to identify the specific activities they will be completing in order to help the organization achieve specific milestones. By identifying these activities, employees see how their specific contributions help to meet the end goal. Also, as employees fill in detail, it helps describe work that still needs doing, and establishes realistic timelines for completion. Many project teams experience difficulty because the volume of work associated with a specific activity has been underestimated, which puts the project off schedule. When important projects fall behind, everyone feels the pressure and lack of achievement.

Another way to achieve forward momentum among employees is to enlist them in reviewing the detailed plan for completion. This helps create ownership for the plan's successful execution and identifies potential areas of concern (such as overoptimistic deadlines). At this stage of the process, ask:

- What will help us overcome the challenges that have been identified?

- What activity is missing?

- What will we need to accomplish to know we have been successful at addressing this issue?

When reviewing the plan, identify what needs to be addressed to successfully execute the change. The concerns that employees identify provide valuable information for anticipating and addressing issues before they become significant obstacles to project completion.

Whenever I talk about "mobilizing forward momentum for project completion," someone generally raises the notion of employee resistance to change. As I articulated in *Done Deal* (Page, 2006),

> *It's vital to lay some groundwork for change to avoid em-*
> *ployee resistance. People resist change for several reasons,*
> *including parochial self-interest, misunderstanding or lack*
> *of trust, different assessments and low tolerance for change.*
>
> *How can you help prepare an organization for change?*
> *Two options include polling and surveying the employee*

population, and developing information and communication strategies aimed at introducing opportunities for employees to participate in the change process. (p. 28)

What concerns me most is employee passivity. That's when I begin to wonder how many previous efforts at change have been cancelled, or how often, maybe due to a change in leadership, what seemed important one day was not the next. Passivity can indicate fatigue with change.

Traditionally, leaders assumed they needed to manage employee resistance to motivate employees during change, but I've since come to realize that resistance is a powerful message that tells me a change initiative has touched on something about which people care deeply. My work has taught me that resistance is a form of energy to lean into, understand and leverage to support the change. When employees articulate a level of resistance, I get curious, ask questions, then "listen." My goal is to understand the employee's deeper issue of concern. Could it be job security, loss of influence, worries about customer impact or the sense that the project will not achieve its desired objective? I listen to determine the underlying concern, then weigh whether it is limited to one person, one group or one department or if it affects the whole organization. Employees who risk sharing what worries them are trying to get a sense of whether their concerns will be heard and addressed. Does what they have to say matter to the organization? Employees are the individuals most closely connected to the unintended consequences of the change. Dealing with the details mobilizes the greatest forward momentum. I often remind my clients, "It's the thousand little steps that help us achieve completion." The challenge is understanding which of those little steps is causing difficulty and what adjustment will diminish or remove the difficulty so the organization can continue to make progress.

Honoring Progress

We live in a world where we are so preoccupied with what still needs to be accomplished that we forget to stop and acknowledge what has already been achieved. I often talk about the "chronic next" world we live in during workshop presentations. Before we pat ourselves on the back for having accomplished something important, we focus on the "next" goal. Take time to honor the progress that is being made as the project moves along. Many different groups will be in the spotlight at various stages of the project. I recall a comment by a participant in a two-day change leadership workshop, who as she was leaving talked about her commitment to buying a package of thank-you cards to thank key champions of a change that they had just completed. The reminder to acknowledge people who contributed to the successful change was a timely one for her. By honoring progress, we encourage group affiliation and community, and recognize everyone's role in the project's success. We must focus attention on those who help bring the project across the finish line. I always ask about the important people who, along the way, enabled the project to get to the final stages. The metaphor that comes to mind for me is a stage performance. The actors are supported by set designers, costume designers, musicians, the director, the producer, makeup artists and a host of people who have a role to play in supporting the actors deliver a superb performance. Honoring progress for me, is about identifying, acknowledging, and supporting the many people along the way who help the project achieve completion.

Then everyone becomes part of the team celebrating. In our drive to identify "next" we often forget to take a moment or two to celebrate progress toward completion. Honoring progress is a wonderful strategy for creating moments of celebration and restoration in the larger, more complex change projects that take months or years to complete.

Celebrating Achievement

Organizations often downplay the importance of celebrating project completion. Helping employees take time to celebrate what has been accomplished before moving forward with the next project, instills breathing space to honor the significant work everyone has done. Too often, organizations leave projects incomplete and employees experience the uncertainty of the project "that never ends." It can be demoralizing to have a project that remains incomplete, especially when it was initiated with fanfare about the strategic importance of the change to the organization. Employees pay attention to actions and behaviors, so completion becomes a symbolic and tangible strategy for acknowledgment.

Earlier in this chapter, I articulated the various opportunities for having mini-celebrations that can help maintain motivation and momentum for final project completion. We know we have arrived at project completion if we have a picture of what "complete" looks like. I encourage change teams to accumulate the criteria for completion early on in the process. As outlined earlier, a definition of project completion can vary greatly among stakeholders. However, collected criteria can serve as a completion checklist invaluable for identifying risks and issues delaying completion. They also give stakeholders a clear picture of the steps required for completion.

Celebrating achievement is such a crucial time for the organization. Organizational cultures are developed through leaders' and employees' actions and behaviors over time. In our personal lives, ritual events acknowledge birthdays, weddings, anniversaries and death.

Organizations benefit greatly from developing intentional rituals for what will be celebrated and acknowledged. To create a culture that supports and enables change projects, establish a ritual for declaring a project complete. Celebrating project completion helps employees recognize that the organization values and acknowledges those who help the organization navigate change.

Too often we diminish the importance of celebrating completion. We talk about not having the time or the money to do it properly, and then it never gets done. This message is being heard loud and clear by employees working to help the organization navigate the change. A heartfelt intentional acknowledgment of employees and the work they do takes commitment and planning. It does not have to take a lot of time or money. As you look at your organization, identify what was recently celebrated. Get curious about what messages these celebrations or lack of celebrations offer employees about what the organization values. As leaders, we play a role in shaping what our workplaces value and what we celebrate. What would you like your organization to be known for valuing and celebrating? What message do you want employees to take away from these celebrations?

Honoring Completion

In honoring completion, the staff at a hiring center marked the beginning of their change initiative with two artifacts.

First, they created a time capsule to be opened following the introduction of their new process. For example, employees included notes of the activities they would no longer need to complete once the new process was in place. They also made notes of the things to which they were saying good-bye. For example, with the new process and system, they would be completing hiring activities in a more streamlined way, not filling jobs one by one.

The second artifact the staff created involved the use of note paper that resembled a quilt. Because quilts get passed down from generation to generation, this note paper represented what employees wanted to keep doing in the future—for example, offering great customer service.

Shared by: Kim Turner, Manager of Strategic Services with the hiring center at the BC Public Service Agency

Completion self-assessment questions:

- What outcomes did we identify at the beginning of the project to help us define completion?

- What activities are we using to motivate momentum?

- What milestones have we identified?

- What opportunities for celebrating key milestones exist?

- What data, artifacts or historical data do we wish to preserve for the completion acknowledgment celebration?

Completion principles:

- Seek opportunities to acknowledge progress toward completion.

- Document and communicate progress.

- Identify the end point that will mark completion early in the project.

- Describe what "done" looks like in terms of outcomes for stakeholders.

Completion action steps:

1. Develop 90-day plans to maintain visibility of progress toward completion.

2. Create a roles and responsibility matrix (example in Chapter 8) to facilitate role clarity in support of overall change progress.

3. Regularly review progress to identify potential risks to completion. Accountability reviews can also facilitate completion.

4. Acknowledge milestone achievement.

Part Two

"Most companies, however, are overly specialized to the particular environment they happen to operate in—especially if they are successful—and then start to lose the ability to change."

—*Paul Schoemaker*

Chapter 7 • The Counter Cs Revealed: "When Change is Stuck, the Counter Cs are Thriving"

"People will forget what you said, people will forget what you did, but people will never forget how you made them feel."

—*Maya Angelou*

The Impact of the Counter Cs: Why Do They Matter?

What happens when good intentions, hectic schedules, multiple priorities, a crisis in the business, change in leadership, a downturn in the economy or one of a multitude of other reasons result in limited or poor execution of the 5Cs? When this happens we experience the Counter Cs.

Table 2. The 5 Cs and Counter Cs

5Cs	Counter Cs
Communication	Concealment
Confidentiality	Contempt
Cultural Compatibility	Callous Disregard
Courtship	Coercion
Completion	Confusion

The Communication Counter C: Concealment

Too often everyone involved with the change gets busy working on "the planning" and "the doing" of the change, and as a result, communicating the change falls off the priority list. The unintended consequence is that employees perceive the organization to be engaged in concealment. Clients are always quick to point out to me that they do not wake up every morning saying, "What am I going to conceal from employees today?" However, if the leadership of the organization is not actively communicating, employees will conclude that the leadership knows what is happening, but is choosing not to communicate. This pattern fuels the perception that the leader is engaging in concealment. In the absence of open communication, the impact on employees, stakeholders, and the organization is profound.

When leaders stifle communication either verbally or nonverbally, employees view feedback or input as unwelcome. The unfortunate result is problems that could benefit from early intervention and ideas that could propel the change initiative are not communicated to the leader. The leader loses touch with employees, the issues and the problems associated with change. Ultimately, both productivity and employee morale suffer. Barwise and Meehan (2008) advocate the regular use of 360-degree input tools to help leaders collect data on whether or not their employees perceive them as welcoming feedback on all aspects of the business and determine where differences in communication effectiveness may exist. These 360-degree tools solicit input and feedback from direct reports, peers, and supervisors in an effort to provide leaders with themed feedback from a variety of sources. Most tools used in 360-degree assessments of leaders include an element of assessment on communication. Regular 360-degree assessments offer leaders the opportunity to hear directly and anonymously from direct reports and colleagues about how their communications are being received.

Behaviors that may indicate Concealment:

- Transmission of false information

- Active rumor mill

- Gossip and innuendo

- Employees and management operating for themselves

- Absence of a sense of community in the workplace

- Negative bonding

- Isolation

- Presence of silos within the organization

- Presentation of "assumptions" as fact

I remind leaders that employees are stakeholders and that by keeping the change communications frequent, authentic, and transparent, the organization can mitigate the issues of lost productivity, lower morale, and reduced retention. When organizational leaders involved in change initiatives wake up every morning, the question they need to ask themselves is, "What can I communicate today?"

Several issues can distract organizations from their goal to communicate openly with employees. Here are potential pitfalls to avoid. First, top management may be reluctant to provide incomplete information. Secretan (2010) shared the impact of this,

> *Often, leaders who fall into the habit of using dishonest jargon do so because they are simply blind to the damage it causes. A euphemism designed to "spin" the truth, is one of the subtlest and most insidious forms of lying. When Nokia Siemens Networks laid off 9,000 employees, they issued a press release describing the action as a "synergy-related headcount adjustment goal." Deceptive bafflegab like this demoralizes followers and undermines the credibility of leaders.* (p. 147)

I encourage clients to openly share what they know, unless there is a critical business reason for withholding information for a short period. Langton and Robbins (2007) reported on research that articulated three reasons an environment for rumors arises: "Rumors emerge as a response to situations that are important to us, where there is ambiguity, and under conditions that arouse anxiety" (p. 261). When organizations undergo change, one of the most powerful tools for addressing the counter C of concealment and the rumor mill is to communicate openly. When so many other factors may be outside leaders' control, this one remains available.

Second, during change, management has a tendency to become risk averse due to quickly shifting priorities. As management makes announcements and then changes decisions, managers become less willing to communicate freely and openly. The desire for "certainty" and the "right answer" results in less and less information. Certainty, after all, is difficult to achieve. Leaders are accustomed to speaking with confidence and certainty during normal business operations. If change is our new "normal," then adopting a consistent communication approach that works during periods of change serves leaders well. Even if the information is unclear or imprecise, that uncertainty can be shared with employees. Choosing to communicate, even in the absence of full information, helps avoid the pitfall of concealment.

Third, during periods of change, key messages can get lost. As leaders, our important role is to distill key messages and time the dissemination of information as it is relevant to employees. For example, being able to respond to issues that directly impact employees' working conditions and status is the first priority in change communications. If the information is readily available, it is key to provide a process and timeline for delivering this information if we wish to help employees navigate the organizational change successfully.

Fourth, traditional communication networks may change. The project leader for the change initiative often becomes the key source of information about the project. Without adjusting communication networks, the organization runs the risk of messages missing key people such as managers not directly involved with the project. Creating change-specific communication networks, such as an intranet home page for the change initiative, minimizes the likelihood of information gaps.

Finally, employees want to know that the leaders are being authentic in their communication. Authenticity comes across when leaders are able to connect their head and heart and lead from the heart as they open their communication. In *Healing the Wounds* David Noer (1993) said speaking from the heart is especially important if the change message is a difficult one. When their leader speaks from the heart, employees do not perceive him or her to be concealing things. I encourage leaders to communicate connection above and beyond content. For example, if the change message is difficult, the opening can be as simple as, "I have a difficult message to communicate today and this period of time in the organization is difficult for all of us." Noer asserted that employees will not connect with the rationale and content if they haven't heard the leader connecting to the heart of the message first. As one employee commented, "Tell us something that sounds like it's coming from someone's heart and not from their ledger" (p. 80). Employees need to know there is a person behind the message being communicated in order to avoid the perception of concealment.

The Confidentiality Counter C: Contempt

When Confidentiality isn't honored or respected, the consequence is mistrust. Employees feel they are being treated with Contempt. When someone feels that a colleague has shared what was supposed to have been a private conversation, that individual loses trust in their confidante and the larger work environment. They feel vulnerable, isolated, unsafe and fearful, which leads to lost productivity as individuals spend energy worrying about and trying to deal with trust issues (Ryan & Oestreich, 1998).

As Kahane (2010) said,

> What holds us back from exercising all of our power and all of our love? Fear. Because we are afraid of offending or hurting others, we hold back our purposefulness and our power. Because we are afraid of being embarrassed or hurt, we hold back our openness and our love. We dysfunction-ally allow our fears to prevent us from becoming whole. (p. 132)

Ryan and Oestreich (1998) weighed in on mistrust toward HR practitioners in particular,

> *The HR department may be thought of as simply an en-*
> *forcement mechanism or a conduit back to line-manage-*
> *ment, causing employees to worry that seeking advice or*
> *counsel will only lead to repercussions. For those with le-*
> *gitimate concerns who need assistance from HR special-*
> *ists, this results in a feeling of being trapped and fearful or*
> *alone.* (p. 72)

Honoring confidentiality builds trust, reduces fear and creates space for hope to blossom. Unfortunately, when we compromise trust, the consequence is decreased trust, increased fear and decreased hope. Is it any surprise that employees experience this as contempt?

Employees who experience contempt feel heightened levels of anxiety, betrayal and disrespect, which negatively impacts the organization. I encourage leaders to invite dialogue and respect the confidentiality of what is shared to minimize these negative impacts. Listening is a very powerful tool for helping leaders mitigate the impact of this counter C.

Ryan and Oestreich (1998) made this point clearly,

> *People want work environments where they are valued as*
> *individuals, where they can learn and contribute, where*
> *they feel they can be most useful and will be treated as*
> *adults. They want to feel good about themselves and have*
> *the chance to be themselves by openly bringing their unique*
> *strengths, skills and intelligence to their work. They want*
> *to be proud of what they do, where they work and who they*
> *work for. Fear undermines all this and in so doing, it leaves*
> *people feeling belittled, cynical, disenfranchised and under-*

standably self protective. Fear makes people smaller—and less capable—than they really are. (p. 45)

Behaviors that may indicate Contempt:

- Silence

- Fear

- Suppressing issues

- Withdrawal

- Withholding

- Leaving

- Bare minimum work performance

- Limited challenging of power

Efforts to avoid experiencing the counter C of contempt begin with building knowledge in the organization for understanding transition. Also important is helping leaders and managers develop the capacity for supporting employees going through transition. Listen and honor what people are sharing with you. In essence, respecting confidentiality creates space for people feeling emotional or lost. As well, avoid the temptation of labeling people as they go through their transition process. Leaders prepared to help and support employees, build organizational resilience and trust. Coaching employees through these transitions is critical. Trustful employees experience greater loyalty and productive energy toward serving the organization's goals.

The Cultural Compatibility Counter C: Callous Disregard

Organizations moving change forward set out to make the organization better. The unintended consequence of a nonconsultative culture results in the experience of callous disregard on the part of employees. Just one infamous email, memo or comment can be recounted again and again. A determination to get through change can make people feel like expendable resources.

Too often, the first employees hear about a new program is when it is publicly announced. If you've ever worked for a branch or regional office, and received a memo about the corporate rollout of a new program, you remember feeling uninvolved, disregarded and disrespected. It looks like corporate headquarters doesn't know or care that the memo conveys a lack of trust in employees outside of corporate headquarters.

When we implement change initiatives without involving employees, particularly in the area of cultural compatibility, the impact is significant.

One example that surfaced during my work revolved around an employee meeting. At this meeting, the executive announced the changes and articulated the likely impact on employees—including, but not limited to, working hours and processes. There was no invitation for employee input, and no Q&A session offered. Instead, shortly after the meeting, managers erected posters announcing the pending change. Just as quickly, employees protested their lack of being consulted by silently removing the posters. That activity stopped when leaders invited staff to a series of meetings and asked them to help shape the pending change.

Behaviors or evidence that may indicate Callous Disregard:

- Open competition

- Missing strengths

- Missing opportunity to learn

- Harassment

- Poisoned work environment

- Stagnation

- Strife

- No dialogue

What strategies are available to avoid having employees experience callous disregard? First, honor what is in the culture and when possible, use the stories of how the culture came to be to prepare for adaptation and change. Second, involve employees when possible, as this will create opportunities for input and feedback and a sense of ownership during a period of time when employees often feel powerless. Finally, pay careful attention to signs of resistance, particularly in the area of cultural change, because this means you've hit on something that matters deeply to people and it is time to lean in and listen carefully. Often, the issues that concern people and the organization differ. Use polarity management, as I shared earlier, to honor both viewpoints without destroying the culture. Also, I invite you to audit the presence of the motivational needs and drives discussed in Chapter 4 on cultural compatibility. Which does your organization need more of to create a culture in which employees can perform and thrive?

The key message: If you wish to avoid the impact of callous disregard, honor the people, which in turn honors the culture many of them participated in creating.

The Courtship Counter C: Coercion

Creating successful change involves positive influencing, persuading and inspiring. So, when does the shadow side of courtship show up—the counter C of coercion—and how might it impact the organization and the change project? What happens when organizational courtship goes sideways and everything we set out to achieve is suddenly in difficulty?

Sometimes, it's the "un"-emotionally intelligent executive who stops by to see how things are going and makes one off-hand remark that causes no end of employee anxiety. Perhaps it's the manager who fails to attend a single change management meeting, telling his department that "we don't have time to do that; we have other priorities." There is both an art and science to change leadership that leaders can benefit from paying attention to. In their article the "Rhythm of Change Leadership," Kerber and Buono (2018) discussed the importance of adaptation; "The change leadership approach varied at different stages of the change process creating a rhythm of change" (p. 57). For these authors rhythm can be defined as a strong, regular, repeated pattern of movement. As such, there are probably multiple, prototypical change leadership rhythms appropriate to different business situations (p. 59).

In the difficult situations articulated above, the unintended consequence of a misaligned leadership approach is employees hearing the misalignment, assuming someone is not telling the truth, and concluding that someone is trying to coerce them into doing something that will ultimately hurt them in some way. I am reminded of David Noer's

(1993) description of the old employment contract in *Healing the Wounds* as "the psychological contract that implies that employees who perform and fit into the culture can count on a job until they retire or choose to leave" (p. 14). This Noer contrasted with the new employment contract: "Even the best performer or the most culturally adaptive person cannot count on long-term employment. It replaces loyalty to an organization with loyalty to one's work" (p. 13). The net impact is the perception of the "throwaway employee." If employees feel they are expendable, you will see the results of coercion in action. How productive do we believe employees will be when they are concerned about job viability?

Removing command, control, coercion and other limiting behaviors from our organizations is hard work. As Margaret Wheatley (2005) highlighted in *Finding Our Way: Leadership for an Uncertain Time*,

> *Enough people drive to work wondering how they can get something done despite the organization—despite the political craziness, the bureaucratic nightmares, the mindless procedures blocking their way. Those leaders who have used participation and self organization have witnessed the inherent desire that most people have to contribute to their organizations.* (p. 67)

Leaders rarely say, "I'm off to coerce someone today." However, when we can't articulate the "why" behind a change initiative, employees text each other, "They know, but they just aren't telling us because the news is bad" or "Management doesn't care about us; they just want us to implement the new system so that our jobs can be moved to a cheaper market." As Secretan (2010) offered, "If we understand ourselves, and if we understand our energy preferences, we will be able to use them to inspire all people—not just some, and not just because we want to manipulate them" (p. 71).

The energy it takes to translate an edict from corporate headquarters into a meaningful strategic response for their employees, typically takes half as much time as responding to all the rumors that get transmitted when a strategy is articulated poorly.

Behaviors or evidence that may indicate Coercion:

- Increased competitiveness

- Hoarding of information and intellectual property

- "Feeding" the rumor mill

- Anger

- Powerlessness

- Fear

- Betrayal

- Resentment

- Negative bonding

Mitigating the counter C of coercion involves proactive leadership, emotional intelligence and clarity of strategy. First, ensure that the change initiative has a credible leader with strong relationships in the organization. Work quickly to rebuild momentum for the change initiative if coercion has taken place.

Second, build emotional intelligence in the leadership team. It is the emotionally intelligent leader who will be able to sense an undercurrent of emotion that needs to be surfaced and addressed, who will be able to remain grounded during difficult meetings with employees, and who will seek out the feedback opportunities so they can become better and more effective at what they offer.

Finally, if the clarity of the strategy has been lost, then regroup, recommit, and address any of the challenges and concerns that are resulting in the experience of mixed messages.

If employees aren't clear about the "why," expect little forward momentum on their part. When they detect ambiguity and uncertainty, employees' willingness to participate falters. And if deep inside you are saying, "They need to follow me because it's their job to do what I say," then I have failed to convince you of the importance of organizational courtship to the success of your change initiative.

Further inspiration comes from, Patrick McCarthy (as cited in Sipe & Frick, 2009), who said, "A relationship is everything. It's a heart experience. Most companies are head experiences – bean counters are running them. When the heart is running them, it becomes exciting" (p. 167). McCarthy reminded me that relationships matter and the leader who fully honors courtship is also sustaining and nurturing the relational web that is so important to organizations that are navigating one change after another.

The Completion Counter C: Confusion

When we take on multiple change projects, begin one project before another is complete or layer too many modifications onto an existing change project, employees experience confusion. Organizational confusion becomes pervasive and leads to diminished productivity. As Barry Johnson (2003) explained in *The Many Facets of Leadership,*

We keep starting one thing after another and never finish any of them. We are overwhelmed and frustrated with unfinished projects all over the place. ... We need to choose a few projects and make sure they are completed. Then people wouldn't be so overwhelmed and would have a sense of completion and accomplishment. (p. 141)

Someone offered the above lament to Barry Johnson as he was addressing a client CEO about initiating projects that went uncompleted. Johnson used their frustration as a strategy for helping them understand the role of the CEO. According to Johnson (2003), "The goal is to be at the upside of Being Expansive and at the upside of Being Focused, which move in combination toward Effective Leadership" (p. 143). Other polarities may be "pulling" your organization away from completion and this is one example of a polarity in action that was having an adverse affect on the organization's ability to achieve completion.

In the absence of organizational clarity, confusion and mixed messages run rampant about what the organizational priorities are and what it will take to achieve them. Employees metaphorically throw up their hands and await word on what current priorities are before acting. Organizations in this predicament have difficulty moving their organization forward. As we all know, keeping something moving or helping it adjust course is one thing, but starting it from a standstill takes more effort, time and care.

Behaviors or evidence that may indicate Confusion:

- Time management problems
- Withdrawal

- Acting out

- Burnout

- High stress

- Second guessing

- Lack of focus

- Cynicism

- Exhaustion

- Unhappiness

- Dissatisfaction

- Frustration

- Loss of sense of accomplishment

- Disappointment

Completion offers employees a sense of value in the work they and the organization do. Incomplete projects devalue employees' work and diminish their trust in identified priorities. Who hasn't experienced the frustration of an incomplete project?

Employees drive themselves toward certainty and seek to reduce ambiguity. A string of incomplete projects leaves them wondering if the organization knows what its priorities are and has the capacity to act on them. Eventually, employees will leave for environments with opportunities for closure and completion.

Chapter 8 • 5C Model Highlights and Tools for Implementation

Change Happens wouldn't be complete without some specific tools to support the work of leveraging each of these dimensions. As I mentioned in the Conclusion section of Chapter 1, there is no one right way to begin using the 5C Model. When people ask me where to start, I suggest at the C where the organization is experiencing its greatest need. For example, if employees sense a lack of communication about the change initiative, then the leadership team should work first on strengthening communication. The following activities are designed to create high involvement during change. May the tools and resources offered below add to your toolkit as you seek to access and leverage the human dimension of change in your organization.

The 5C Model: Dimension 1 • Communication

As we examine strengthening the communication C in our change efforts, here are some high-value activities to get you started. As you may recall, communication is the open, honest, frequent and strategic sharing of relevant information.

Develop a Communication Plan. Elements to include:

- Identify the key messengers.

- Ensure key messengers have the information they need.

- Develop the key messages.

- Identify the key messaging vehicles: road show, email, blog, stand-up meetings, management meetings.

- Set the key milestone dates.

- Identify the key stakeholders receiving the communications.

- Develop the schedule for communication.

Assess the Communication protocol. Evaluate how to adapt the existing communication protocol so both change and routine communications can be timely and relevant.

Develop a communication accountability protocol. Consider how to best set up communication channels that ensure all employees receive information from their managers in a 72-hour period. Identify the accountability protocol if a department or unit has not received the communication pertaining to the change program in the established time period. Navigating the Communication C requires each manager to promote accountability for communication in their department and to follow through on their commitments to their people and their organization. In particular, during periods of change, uncertainty is common, and strong consistent communication practices will provide significant relief.

Develop feedback mechanisms for soliciting and receiving input from employees. It may be as simple as asking these straightforward questions at a "town hall" style meeting: "What information do you need that you don't have? What questions remain unanswered for you that would help you perform your role more effectively? What can I do for you in terms of communication that I'm not already doing?" Other tools include online survey tools such as SurveyMonkey, as well as pulse checks and diagnostic interviews by a change agent or independent consultant. All offer ways of gaining feedback and input, which in turn give employees an increased sense of ownership and involvement in the change initiative.

Build management communication capacity during a change program. Identify the comfort and communication expertise of the management team and ensure that additional training and learning opportunities are available to support the communication accountability framework. Share a common communication language and offer mentoring, coaching and support to developing communicators.

Develop the communication guiding principles and agreements with the management team. Have a session where the management team participates in negotiating the communication flow and process. The agreements developed, prioritized and agreed to by the management team will offer everyone a clear understanding of effective communication with employees.

Gain and reinforce management commitment throughout the change. Consider offering strategically placed retreats to prepare leaders for communicating the next stage of change. Too often managers begin to feel isolated from the change process as the initiative moves through milestones. Unless there is a problem, they lose a sense of connection to the process. Strategically placed retreats that seek input on upcoming milestones and offer updates on the process ensure that managers are poised for success in the change initiative.

Give all stakeholders a voice in the process. Find multiple ways to offer all stakeholders a person to call or email, to ensure their voices are heard. Remember, communication isn't the message. Seek opportunities to hear what else stakeholders wish to share.

The 5C Model: Dimension 2 • Confidentiality

The Confidentiality C seeks to honor the need to respect the confidentiality of individual situations and employees' reactions to the change initiative. So much of honoring confidentiality involves our intention on this front. The following ideas offer ways to make a visible impact regarding confidentiality.

Have an open door and a closed mouth. Create multiple opportunities to communicate to employees that there are places they can connect to share their concerns with the change initiative. A confidentiality support chain might include the manager or supervisor, designated HR practitioner, the Employee Assistance Program contact and key members of the project team chosen for their ability to honor confidentiality and respect information that individuals share.

Honor the absent. Take steps to develop organizational agreements that honor the absent within the organization. Ask individuals who have issues with the change to identify what action they would like you to take. Quite often employees want some action taken, however, they do not wish to be identified with the issue that is being raised. Be mindful to differentiate between issues to be addressed and people that are being complained about in the process. If the individual raising the issue would like to see it elevated to the point it will be addressed, ensure the protocols are in place to do that. If, however, someone complains about a colleague, that calls for an approach that offers the individual the tools to address the situation directly, or to raise the issue with their supervisor. That may mean closing a conversation that appears to be headed toward a complaint about an individual, or switching to a coaching role that empowers the individual to address the situation directly. To avoid what is called "triangulation," avoid being left holding the responsibility for raising the complaint about another individual on behalf of the person who approached you. It's a sticky situation that can contribute to mistrust in the organization.

Develop a transition management plan. As discussed in Chapter 3 which explored the confidentiality C, there are two processes unfolding for employees. The first is navigating the external change and the second is navigating the internal psychological process of transition, as identified by William Bridges (2003). In order to honor the transition process that takes place, I encourage change agents and change leaders to develop transition management plans that help employees navigate Bridges's (2003) three phases of transition: endings, the neutral zone, and new beginnings. For more information, add a copy of Bridges's book, *Managing Transitions: Making the Most of Change,* to your resource library.

Offer transition workshops. Employees are often challenged by their colleagues' varied responses and feel isolated by their own conflicting reactions. Transition workshops let them see themselves in the transition process and identify what is unfolding for them. They can better identify their unmet needs and get the support required to navigate the process. I refer to the change process as offering a container for normalizing the reactions people are having by presenting a context.

Management modeling of trustworthy behavior. During change initiatives, stresses and challenges unfold for both employees and management. Management needs a support system in place and needs to model behavior important to the process. For example, identify organizational agreements like "honor the absent" and "respect confidentiality," key trust-building behaviors during the initiative. Further encouragement for engaging in dialogue that identifies the specific behaviours that support agreements and values within organizations comes from Brown (2018), who stated, "Only about 10 percent of organizations have operationalized their values into teachable and observable behaviors that are used to train their employees" (p. 190). What a significant lost opportunity for engaging employees in conversations that matter before, during, and after change.

Respect confidentiality. The single most important behavior that managers and change practitioners can exhibit is a respect for confidentiality. By not naming individuals who are struggling, the positive impact is that people who are present to these conversations feel reassured that if they experience a difficulty in the project, they likely will not be named either.

Acknowledge the challenge inherent in change. Change is uncomfortable and it is relentless. We change because we risk becoming irrelevant with the status quo. I invite change leaders to share the context of "why this change is needed now" as a way of introducing and acknowledging the challenges that the change will bring and to explicitly identify the sources of support that exist for employees who experience challenges and issues with the change.

The 5C Model: Dimension 3 • Cultural Compatibility

Cultural Compatibility speaks to the importance of aligning an organization's values, beliefs and principles. Rarely does a change project not require actively managing and shifting prevailing cultural values. Below are tools for doing so.

Identify the culture keepers. The culture keepers play a key role in helping change agents identify the sacred elements of the culture. They help explain how particular aspects of the culture showed up in the organization and what the greatest challenges will be as stakeholders navigate needed shifts in the culture.

Begin by acknowledging the cultural strengths that already exist. Too often when change agents and leaders embark on a project, they want to move it into high gear without first acknowledging the culture that got them to where they are today. Begin with acknowledging the current strengths and leverage these to help the organization move forward with the change.

Actively manage cultural compatibility. Two departments can have very different cultural norms and values. The cultural compatibility C simply highlights the importance of actively managing cultural compatibility between partners within an organization, which need to come together to support the change initiative. The saying "we're all one happy family" won't do it for organizations seeking a successful change outcome.

Conduct cultural due diligence. Take time to identify the similarities and differences between the current and desired culture.

To help you conduct your own cultural due diligence, identify the following:

- The reward approaches used
- The behaviors of recognized leaders
- How decisions are made
- Significant leaders and people the organization promotes and rejects
- The type of successes the organization experiences
- The type of errors the organization makes

- How stakeholder relationships are managed

- The use of power in the organization

- What is important, rewarded or punished

- How people relate to each other, solve conflict and deal with success and failure

Conduct new leader integration meetings. Many companies such as Adobe and Cisco have adopted and refined this practice. It involves meetings that offer an incredible opportunity for employees to share what is important to them about the organization, while creating space for new leaders to learn about and honor the new department or organization they are joining. It also offers a great opportunity for newly hired leaders to share their philosophy, experiences, and leadership approach. Ask employees to a meeting where they have the opportunity to respond to the following questions. Then collate their input on key questions of culture for the new leader. After pulling together the information, invite the new leader to respond to employee questions and to share their perspectives and leadership philosophy. Provide a facilitator internal to the organization to help employees prepare the information and facilitate the dialogue when the leader joins the conversation. For additional resources for new leaders, please see Watkin's (2013) book, *The First 90 Days*.

Questions for employees:

- What do we already know about _____ (name of leader)?

- What would we like to know about the leader?

111

- What does the leader need to know about us as a team?

- What do we want most from the leader?

- What are our concerns with this individual becoming our leader?

- What is going well in the organization that energizes us?

- What are the major problems or challenges we will be facing?

- What suggestions do we have to overcome the above concerns?

- How can we help _____ overcome these problems?

Questions for a new leader:

- How would teams you have led in the past describe what it is like to work with you?

- What parts of your job do you like the best? The least?

- What are your top three priorities over the next 6 months for this team?

- What do you expect of this team?

- How will people know if their performance is not meeting your requirements?

- How do you make decisions?

- How is it best to share information with you?

- How often will this team meet? What social information would be good for this team to know? Hobbies? Interests? Passions?

Articulate a compelling vision that incorporates the organization's cultural strengths. How have these strengths played a role in helping the organization achieve the proper positioning for this change?

Be mindful of symbolic opportunities to honor the culture and support the change. Identifying opportunities to represent and honor the change symbolically can help employees make the leap between the past and the future. What symbols are important to your organization? How might they help leverage the overall change effort?

One of the tools that supports cultural transformation is the work of the Barrett Values Centre. The suite of cultural transformation tools helps organizations strengthen and align organizational, employee and management team values. See the Internet Resources section for more information.

The 5C Model: Dimension 4 • Courtship

Courtship is the "why" of this change initiative—the vision, the strategy and the reason. As change leaders and practitioners move deeper into a change project, the lever of courtship sometimes gets lost in the midst of the "doing" of the change project activities. Below are ideas designed to maintain the momentum and leverage courtship throughout the project.

Complete the stakeholder assessment: This grid developed by Worley et al. (1996) allows you to assess the level of support among key stakeholders by name (p. 119).

Table 3. Grid to Assess Stakeholders' Level of Support

Stakeholder (Name)	Active Resistance	Passive Resistance	Passive Support	Active Support

After you complete the grid, identify one action step for each individual that will move the stakeholder toward greater support for the change initiative. We change the world one conversation at a time, and I recommend completing this grid quarterly as a way to continue to monitor the shifts being experienced.

Recognize that the courtship never ends. If as leaders we recognize that we are "courting" employees before and during a change—as well as to prepare for the next change—we've got the essence of this C. The moment we shift away from this approach, we run the risk of taking actions that diminish employee engagement and ownership for the change effort.

Avoid telling. Unfortunately, many leaders let everyone know that this is their job and they get paid for doing it. Whenever possible, I encourage leaders to "sell, don't tell." That way employees appreciate that a rationale exists for the change and they feel encouraged to participate and help its success. The moment leaders choose to "mandate" the change, employees lose heart and motivation. I have experienced this time and time again.

Involve employees in identifying improvements. Seek opportunities for including employees in the change. I recommend that change leaders include employees whenever possible, especially when decisions might impact the nature of their work. Too often, leaders and change practitioners find it more expedient to make the decisions themselves, with the net result being that much time is invested persuading people to get on board. The most expedient approach is actually involving people up front in the decisions that affect them.

Develop a compelling answer to the why question. This is the question that will be asked repeatedly throughout the change initiative. Better yet, the question is, "why now?" Leveraging the courtship C involves having an identified strategy to offering a compelling answer the question "why now?" The leadership challenge here is to avoid defaulting to the adage, "because corporate thinks it's important." Part of any leader's challenge is to help develop an appropriate rationale for employees, so that the answer has meaning for them. Developing this rationale is not about ignoring potential pitfalls of the change initiative for your people. Rather, it is about shouldering the leadership responsibility you assumed in service of your people, and ultimately of the organization.

Maintain the spirit of invitation throughout the process. This element of courtship relies significantly on the intention behind every communication and conversation that takes place. As one workshop participant offered, "I get it! A little less marriage and a little more courtship." As change leaders, finding ways to continue to invite people on this change journey requires preparation, patience and actively seeking to identify and communicate the ultimate benefits of the change.

Harness the strengths that already exist in the organization. One clear strategy for maintaining a focus on courtship is to honor and build on the strengths present. Wherever possible, capitalize on what is already in place, so that the change feels less uncertain to the people most directly affected. For example, we can talk about how innovation has supported us in previous change initiatives and, as we move forward, we will be calling on our shared history of innovation.

Assess change readiness. Engaging in change readiness assessments enables employees and the leadership team to become involved in identifying and assessing the risks associated with the change initiative. Assessing the organization's readiness at the systems, process and people levels will provide valuable data for the change management and transition management plans.

The 5C Model: Dimension 5 • Completion

Completion is the acknowledgment of achieving ongoing milestones and intentional closure for the change project. In the spirit of creating completion, I articulate helpful ideas and activities below.

Develop the discipline of 90-day plans. In organizations that don't monitor what gets completed, a culture develops of moving from one thing to the next, which I introduced earlier as the "chronic next" culture. As a result, there is no opportunity to take time to pause and recognize what has been completed. Implementing 90-day plans offers everyone an opportunity to monitor progress against goals and celebrate achievements each quarter. Also, goals not achieved within 90 days can be adjusted and carried forward to the next quarter. The visibility, transparency and accountability that exist as a result of this one practice will see all members through to completion and its celebration.

Create RACI charts. The RACI acronym stands for Responsible, Approve, Consult and Inform. RACI charts add role clarity and accountability to change initiatives. Set up a table (as depicted on the following page) with a list of activities that need to be accomplished as part of a change initiative. Across the top of the table, add the letters RACI in individual columns. Then place the appropriate initials in each of the columns across from the activity. There should be only one set of initials in the approver column and the responsible column. Someone has to have the designated authority for each activity. When there are multiple sets of initials, clarity is lost. The goal is to offer role clarity for specific activities. By revisiting the RACI chart on a regular basis, you offer employees information on who they need to consult if they want to offer or receive information about a specific activity. As Tom Devane (2007) suggested, when we establish clear responsibilities using a RACI chart, everyone knows who is responsible for what, which minimizes duplicate activities and ensures that the unexpected is covered (p. 68).

Table 4. RACI Matrix

Activity	R Responsible	A Approver	C Consult	I Inform
Identify change champions	RB	CM	RB, CM, MP, AP	All employees
Conduct transitions training sessions	AP	RB	MP	All employees
Schedule employee town hall meeting	RB	CM	MP	AP to coordinate
Determine desired change outcomes	CM	ES	Leadership team	All employees

Celebrate completion. Start considering what the celebration will include when you're at the beginning of the project. If you wait until the project's end, you'll lose much of the project's history, particularly on a long-term project. Discussing it early on clearly allows you to begin with the end in mind. What "firsts" can be captured? What photographs can be taken along the way that can serve as mementos at the completion celebration? What key activities need to be honored? Make someone responsible for keeping an "eye on the ball" of completion. That will ensure activity documentation throughout, to capture the project's wholeness and impact.

Keep a running list of the employees who deserve recognition.
Who are the unsung heroes, the contributors without whom the project would not have been completed? What role did informal influencers play at critical moments to achieve its ultimate success? Make sure both the work and people are recognized as the project reaches completion.

Facilitate regular After-Action Reviews. Organizations often carry through a change project without harvesting lessons that could serve future change efforts. After-Action Reviews (AARs) originally developed as a practice in the US Military. Non-military organizations have adapted this process, which seeks to evaluate without blame what happened, and harvest the best practices for future action. The authors of the article "Learning in the Thick of It," offered four questions that form the basis for the AAR: "What were our intended results? What were our actual results? What caused our results? And what will we sustain or improve?" (Darling, Parry, & Moore, 2005, pp. 88–89).

To honor the discipline of the AAR practice, the authors also emphasize the importance of preparing with the end in mind, by discussing the following questions in advance of the initiative: "What are our intended results and measures? What challenges can we anticipate? What have we or others learned from similar situations? What will make us successful this time?" (p. 92). This disciplined practice offers organizations a way to continuously adjust and improve their change efforts.

Solicit customer and client feedback. As projects reach completion, take the time to connect with clients and customers to assess their experience. This becomes a wonderful way to partner with stakeholders,

119

update them on the progress of the project and solicit their views on what is working and what could use improvement. Using this strategy further develops your relationship with external stakeholders and helps solicit their involvement as change initiatives are introduced into the organization. In the spirit of honoring completion, their input can serve as a powerful opportunity to recognize key members in the organization who contributed to the project's success.

Create a time capsule. This activity is designed to begin with the end in mind. At a project's conclusion, having a series of artifacts to review can be wonderful way to capture what has been accomplished and the level of effort involved. Artifacts could include measures of efficiency before the project, the original vision statement for the project and anything else that helps members appreciate what was accomplished.

Chapter 9 • Sustaining Resilience Amidst Change and Values-Based Leadership

Resilience is a hot topic, receiving a lot of research and media attention. Resilience is often seen in workplaces where people feel they belong. Our efforts to cultivate workplaces of belonging (Block, 2008; Stallard & Pankau, 2008) in constantly changing environments are yielding resilience challenges for leaders and employees alike. Resilience positively enhances our ability to handle conflict, our competence for managing everyday stressors, and our capacity for navigating the many relationships we have with employees and stakeholders. Kathryn McEwen (2016), an Australian organizational psychologist, defined resilience as "an individual's capacity to manage the everyday stress of work and remain healthy, rebound and learn from unexpected setbacks and prepare for future challenges proactively" (p. 2). She developed the Resilience at Work (R@W) assessment to help individuals evaluate their level of resilience and establish an action plan for strengthening resilience at work. A study published in 2016 concluded, "A brief workplace-based resilience program was able to significantly improve employee resilience as measured by the RAW Scale" (Rogerson, Meir, Crowley-McHattan, McEwen, & Pastoors, 2016, p. 333). See the Internet Resources section to learn more about Resilience and the R@W assessment.

In a *Globe and Mail* article, Ungar (2019) discussed the importance of resourcing as a factor that contributes to resilience. Ungar suggested, "[Find] the relationships that nurture you, the opportunities to use your talents and the places where you experience community and governmental support and social justice... your world will help you succeed more than you could ever help yourself" (para. 39).

121

I offer this chapter to support you and your leadership practice. Specifically, I present the opportunity to reflect how armored leadership, which Brené Brown (2018) described as defensiveness, posturing, and self-protective behaviors, may be adversely impacting your resilience as a leader.

In 2016, I completed research that examined the role that values play in sustaining leaders as they navigate challenges (Page, 2016). In speaking with these leaders, I began to realize the importance of cultivating leaders who could sustain themselves amidst change and challenge. The following material summarizes some of the key messages from my research. For more information see the *International Journal of Public Leadership* article titled "Public Leadership" (Page, 2016). In this chapter, I explore specific recommendations and opportunities for leaders to sustain themselves and others by integrating the key themes and findings from my 2-year research project into a model that I offer to leaders. I weave in comments from participants while exploring the various aspects of the model more fully. My intention is to put forward a model and honor what participants shared with me in service of current and future leaders.

Leaders have impact (Manz, Anand, Joshi, & Manz, 2008). The impact that they have can potentially be generative or harmful to organizations, the people who report to them, and the public whom they serve. Previous studies of relational and values-based leadership have identified that people have relational values that guide their behaviors and decision making (Diochon & Anderson, 2011; Larson & Hunter, 2014).

This research demonstrated that values play a role in the following three areas: enabling leaders to attend to transitions for themselves and others, building a values-based support network, and exploring personal mastery and learning amidst leadership challenges. In addition, leaders benefit from having conversations about values with their direct reports and colleagues. Finally, engaging in conversations about values is potentially more important than having the same values. The next section explores research elements that support building sustainable leadership capacity for leaders who must navigate inevitable leadership challenges.

Building Sustainable Leadership

I developed the Values Implications for Leaders model based on the research to offer an approach for helping leaders sustain themselves as they navigate challenge. Key themes included leading oneself and others through transitions, cultivating community through a strong values-based support network, and pursuing personal mastery and learning amidst challenge. In the Values Implications for Leaders section following Figure 3, I also relied on the transitions framework of William Bridges (2009), which was previously explored in Chapter 3.

Leading Self and Other Through Transition, Change, and Challenge

Leadership is a process. This research highlighted activities that contribute to sustaining leaders as they navigate challenge. Specifically, as explored in Chapter 3, the transitions zones identified by Bridges (2009) included three zones: endings, neutral zone, and new beginnings. In our action-oriented experience of leadership, transition is often overlooked in organizations. It is essential for leaders to address transitions and to create conversational opportunities to explore and more fully understand these individualized processes of recalibration and reintegration.

The Role of a Strong Values-Based Support Network

As leaders develop and lead employees through the transitions that are associated with change and challenge, it is important to nurture a network of peer support to provide a values-based, nonjudgmental, and listening ear during these periods of personal and professional turbulence. Kralik et al. (2006) stated, "Healthy transitions are often linked to the development of relationships and connections with others" (p. 325). Navigating challenge takes an emotional toll. As Heifetz and Linsky (2002) pointed out, "The most difficult work of leadership involves learning to experience distress without numbing yourself" (p. 227). As challenging as it is, leaders must experience the distress associated with the challenge and use the wisdom in their emotions to help themselves and others. As Brown (2015) noted, "The process of regaining our emotional footing in the midst of struggle is where our courage is tested and our values are forged" (p. xviii). The connection of transitions to the value of courage, is possible when a strong support network that has been nurtured over time is available to leaders when they experience challenge. As participants noted, the leaders who took part in the research benefited from support, which included a strong professional network, a strong personal network, and mentors who might not work in the same department, but who nonetheless served as trusted advisors (Maister, Green, & Galford, 2000). These mentors were available to offer input, guidance, and perspective as leaders confronted challenging situations.

The importance of having a professional support network was reinforced for me as I conducted this research. I recall facilitating two-day workshops on change leadership within a provincial government organization with the uppermost non-appointed leadership group. As I stepped in to work with these leaders, I realized quite quickly that in the previous 3-year period, with limited access to professional development, their professional network as well as their connections among each other had deteriorated. I realized that their presence in the course offered an opportunity to rebuild this fractured network.

Personal Mastery and Learning Amidst Challenge

Personal mastery is challenging ourselves to continually grow in the pursuit of our values. The capacity to choose personal mastery and learning amidst leadership challenges supports leadership sustainability. Over the past several years, I have been struck by the "chronic next" culture that leaders are experiencing. This section holds a special place for me in the research. As an educator and a consultant who seeks to build capacity in people and organizations to function more holistically and productively, the choice for personal mastery and learning amidst challenge is a profound one.

In examining the relationship between navigating leadership challenges and learning, Frost (2014) noted, "Leading values-based organizations is a dynamic process and one that requires people to constantly be learning and evolving their thinking" (p. 125). Specifically, identifying, defining, and refining values within the context of leadership and challenge is an ongoing process of discovery, clarification, and learning. The case for leaders as learners (Kouzes & Posner, 2007) is strong. Senge (2006) described personal mastery as "a relentless willingness to root out the ways we limit or deceive ourselves from seeing what is, and to continually challenge our theories of why things are the way they are" (p. 148). A constant willingness to examine values, understand current context, and explore personal mastery is called for in complex public sector environments. Leaders quickly become disconnected from the very tools that allow them to continue to develop and learn the skills that enable them to continue to serve themselves, those they work with, and the common good.

Moments to pause, reflect, and celebrate accomplishments are occurring less and less as the drive to accomplish the next thing presents itself. Senge (2006) offered, "Those who become lifelong learners become what [Schön] calls 'reflective practitioners.' The ability to reflect one's thinking while acting, for Schön, distinguishes the truly outstanding professionals" (p. 176). The discipline of harvesting learning through reflection is supported in the literature (Etmanski, Fulton, Nasmyth, & Page, 2014; Kiel, 2015; Page & Margolis, 2017; Wood Daudelin, 1996). The public sector requires resilience, renewal, and sustainability. The factors impacting these goals and their interrelationships are shown in Figure 3.

Figure 3. Building sustainable public sector leadership (Page, 2016).

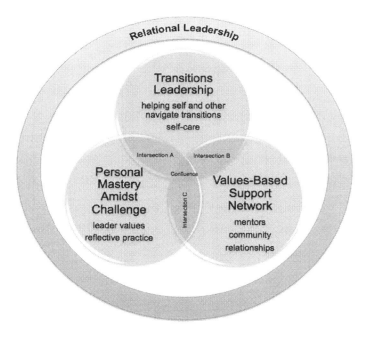

Intersection A: Transitions leadership and personal mastery:
Attending to community to build sustainable human capacity.
Intersection B: Transitions leadership and support network:
Building and implementing sustainable self-care practices.
Intersection C: Personal mastery and support network:
Serving as a model of sustainable leadership in community.
Confluence: Sustained stewards building leadership capacity in self and others: using values to release the hero in everyone.

The three components in Figure 3 intersect with each other, and each intersection requires different leadership. The importance of exploring the role of values for leaders as they navigate challenge contributes to leadership sustainability.

Values Implications for Leaders

While there are varied perspectives on leadership, George, Sims, McLean, and Mayer (2007) asserted strong values-based leadership is critical in today's fast-paced global climate.

Values act as a guidepost in an environment that is in constant change, offering leaders a foundation for decision making. Positive impact is possible when the invitation to operate from guiding values and principles is used to build capacity in others. In our complex organizations, we need leaders who have clarity of the values that guide their work. This will enable leaders to assist others to learn how to engage in generative dialogue and problem solving, rather than coming to their leader for the right answer. Capacity building by incorporating values into day-to-day conversations and problem solving will enable leaders to bring more of themselves to this important and necessary work.

127

Thoughtfully and intentionally cultivating environments in which issues and potential solutions are considered within the context of values offers everyone in the organization the opportunity to participate in generative conversations. The opportunity to deepen and broaden the skillset for considering values can be spread broadly throughout our organizations. The importance of dialogue and exploration of core values in particular is emphasized within the multicultural leadership literature (Bordas, 2012). In exploring the role of values and leadership, Bordas (2012) concluded, "Values are the touchstones for multicultural leadership principles dedicated to building a benevolent and just society that upholds the well-being of all people and nurtures future generations" (p. 24). Leaders have the opportunity to use values to move beyond the impact of short-term, cyclical shifts in our organizations and adopt a longer term mindset.

Relational Leadership, Values, and Community

The literature abounds with leadership advice on building connection and community through values and relationships. As Ospina and Sorenson (2006) noted, "This perspective emphasizes relational processes that depend on social networks of influence, so that leadership is enacted at all levels of the network" (p. 198). Fletcher (2012) emphasized the relationship between leader and follower and stated that over the past several years the "concept of relationality has deepened, become more explicit, and expanded beyond positional leadership to a concept that emphasizes personal leadership regardless of position or organizational role" (p. 85). The relational leadership literature offered additional considerations for leaders who are seeking to build networks, communities of practice, and strengthen collaboration in our highly interconnected world. Specifically, leaders have the opportunity to view relationality as an additional source of leverage.

Values-based leadership offers us the bridge to strengthening our relationships, and ultimately our communities. As Wheatley (2009) stated, "Our pressure-cooked lives are driving us farther away from the very resource that could most help us—strong relationship with those in our local communities" (p. 1). Professional and personal support networks contribute to sustaining leaders as they navigate challenge. Indeed, values-based leadership supports greater connection (Frost, 2014). Perhaps the keys to leadership sustainability exists in building stronger connections and a greater sense of interconnectedness in communities.

The literature on the many benefits of belonging in community is rich (Block, 2008; Stallard & Pankau, 2008; Wheatley, 2009). In particular, Block (2008) defined community as "the experience of belonging. We are in community each time we find a place where we belong" (p. xii). As defined, belonging suggests ownership and feeling as though individuals are a part of something (Block, 2008). Leaders have a significant opportunity to enable employees to experience a greater sense of belonging in their work and in their organizations. The presence of caring or care as a collective value is well represented in the literature (Larson & Murtadha, 2002; Rusaw, 2005). In particular, authors identified care as a value that was grounded in relationships rather than roles (Larson & Murtadha, 2002). In interconnected and interdependent organizations, caring, greater relational connection among individuals, and increasing collaboration to solve complex issues may result in a greater sense of community, which may ultimately foster a sense of collective ownership.

Reflections on the Importance of Values

Through my research I found that the capacity for leaders to engage in dialogue about values is perhaps more important than the specific values that they hold. A key leadership capacity is having values, and being able to share what they are with others. Values can serve as a bridge to building community. By engaging in reflective dialogue about these values with peers, direct reports, and other stakeholders, leaders make available to others important information about what matters to them. This information extends the invitation to others to engage in this meaning making and reflective process. The act of sharing values and engaging in dialogue about these values may be a source of leverage for leaders who are seeking to build community and collective empowerment (Kirk & Shutte, 2004).

Servant leadership is one example that may be of service to leaders who wish to honor the seven-generation rule (Bordas, 2012). As Spears and Laurence (2004) offered, "At its core, servant-leadership is a long-term, transformational approach to life and work—in essence, a way of being—that has the potential for creating positive change throughout our society" (p. 12). This perspective invites leaders to adopt and maintain a stance that is clearly focused on future generations, despite pressure from media, the election cycle, and interest groups to operate differently. As Van Wart (2014) noted, servant leadership promotes the philosophy that "it is the leader who is privileged to serve the people" (p. 34).

As Greenleaf (2008) stated, "The servant-leader is servant first… It begins with the natural feeling that one wants to serve, to serve first. Then conscious choice brings one to aspire to lead" (p. 15). Similarly, within Indigenous leadership literature, the commitment to community is a significant factor that influences leadership selection (Kenny, 2012).

Setting the Stage for Moving Forward

The opportunity to move beyond the model of leadership that reinforces a heroic leader is gaining momentum. A variety of alternatives now exist, which enable leaders to embrace values-based leadership more explicitly as part of their leadership practice. Leadership theorists and values theorists are making contributions to leadership so that these alternatives can be more fully explored in practice. Leadership models that emphasize values include values-based leadership (Barrett, 1998; Copeland, 2014; Frost, 2014; Hall, 2001; O'Toole, 1996), servant leadership (Greenleaf, 1998, 2008; Russell, 2001; Sipe & Frick, 2009; Spears, 2002; Spears & Lawrence, 2004; Van Wart, 2014), virtuous leadership (Bright, Cameron, & Caza, 2006; Cameron, 2011), shared leadership (Amar, Hentrich, & Hlupic, 2009), not to mention the alternative perspectives in leadership literature (Kenny, 2012; Larson & Murtadha, 2002; Sinclair, 2007, 2009; Young Leon, 2012). The above leadership models and frameworks have positive and affirming values embedded in their approach.

My wish is that the vast number of values-based alternatives that exist for leaders will enable them to both sustain themselves and the people they work with as they build capacity for everyone to think, reflect, and act from a values-based perspective. With this approach, not only will decisions be anchored in values, they will also offer individuals the innovation and creativity to take ownership for their decisions and the values that guided them towards the actions they took. Furthermore, they will benefit from other spin-off attributes like trust, resilience, and sustainability

Implications for Leadership

Leading from values is a sacred journey. Leading from values invites others to be part of the journey. Busch and Wennes (2012) noted, "In organisations where the employees enjoy a great deal of autonomy in the execution of their work, it is important to cultivate values which allow them to develop strong bonds of identification with the organisation" (p. 205). When leaders can have transparent conversations about values with the staff that help them achieve their workplace goals, recommendations can be developed within these shared values (Busch & Wennes, 2012; Kouzes & Posner, 2007; Paarlberg & Perry, 2007; Posner, Kouzes, & Schmidt, 1985). What might be possible if people were able to bring problems and recommendations that aligned with shared values to the leaders? Leaders must build capacity in staff to think through issues and engage in values-based decision making and enable them to have challenging conversations about what values are the highest priority in situations where values conflicts emerge. As part of their discussion, Busch and Wennes (2012) noted, "Leaders must become more proficient at handling conflicting values" (p. 211). Furthermore, leaders and employees have additional opportunities to make decisions that rely less on how it would play in the media and more about how it would align with the lived values of the organization and the longer term perspective.

Perhaps the summative comment on the sustaining nature of values comes from a leader I interviewed, who offered,

> *What sustains me as a leader is … being able to work with people when you are working from sort of a values-base. … [It's] being able to work in a group where you start with that place and can build up from it. … [It's] being able to identify*

and recognize and celebrate when people do things that are wonderful like that, when they operate from a values-based approach and a caring approach.

This participant articulated the combination that facilitates leading with heart. Embedding values in the dialogue and expressions of caring as two elements she embraces in her leadership.

I have learned that values matter— leaders have them, leaders talk about them, and leaders share what values mean to them. In doing so, leaders inspire others. Through dialoguing about values, leaders have the opportunity to share their humanity as they experience the challenges that come from a desire to live by their values, even though this sometimes results in values conflicts and compromises. Yet, in choosing to live into values, leaders identify their aspirations and inspire others to do the same. As leaders we need to have serious conversations with ourselves about our values. What do we stand for? We then need to share them with others. We also need to be mindful of the diverse values that exist around us and collaborate with others to identify shared values together. Shared values bring people together. We have much work to do in sharing our values more broadly in service of creating community and a greater sense of belonging. Values create a sense of belonging and serve as the bridge to building community.

As Ferdig (2007) noted, "We must first acknowledge sustainability challenges, learn their origin and meaning, and then develop appropriate skills and courses of action to meet those challenges" (p. 30). What if the very sustainability challenge that needs to be addressed is leadership sustainability? Values can play a role in sustaining leaders as the speed and pace of change continues to accelerate. Leaders operating from core values will have the opportunity to create space to nurture the leader within the many communities in their sphere of responsibility. Rather than choosing one or the other, Wheatley (2005) offered guidance on the power of both-and thinking: "Life requires the honoring of its two great needs, not one. In seeking to be a community member, we cannot abandon our need for self-expression" (pp. 48–49). Greater possibilities exist within leadership to honor oneself and others, rather than others at the expense of oneself, or vice versa.

I also learned that there are fabulous leaders who are learning how to sustain themselves and others as they navigate the inevitable challenges that come with leadership. Harvesting the wisdom from their stories offered me an opportunity to share the lessons learned with others in service of building our collective leadership capacity for sustaining ourselves.

Chapter 10 • What Next?

The 5C Model has existed since 2004. The first book, *Done Deal* resulted from a combination of research with consultants and researchers. Since then I have facilitated workshops with thousands of participants, developed a 6-month change agent certificate program, been retained to help implement the 5C Model, facilitated leadership development sessions, and engaged in ongoing thinking and reflecting on the 5C Model. The second edition of this book is an integration of my ongoing learning and experience with the model. I have learned that it invites people to think differently about change. If change projects focus on leveraging the value of the human dimension, then the model guides practitioners and leaders to access human possibility in a way that accelerates change efforts.

The 5C Model is intended to offer you practical wisdom on navigating change in a way that unifies rather than dismantles your people, your work groups and your organizations. By remaining whole and together, employee engagement can be maintained and even strengthened during change. It begs the question, what would be possible for our organizations if there was no significant "lost productivity effect" experienced as a result of change? Models help us see what we might not otherwise consider. As a client once said,

> *Our project was complex; there were lots of pieces to it, and the 5C Model helped us develop integrated thinking about the whole system... Whenever you engage in a model like this you are engaging in systems thinking!*

When we undertake to lead change we must consider whole systems. This is a fundamental skill set for change managers. For exercising your systems thinking muscles further, I recommend *Thinking in Systems* by Danella Meadows (2008) and *Growing Wings on the Way: Systems Thinking for Messy Situations* by Rosalind Armson (2011).

So, What Next?

As part of our conversation about honoring the human dimension while navigating change, I use the Organization Behavior (OB) model as a frame for articulating shifts needed by individuals, groups and organizations. The OB model offers us a framework to look at organizations at three levels: the individual, group or team and organizational systems (see Figure 4). The OB model articulates shifts needed for leaders who use the 5C model to facilitate more successful change. As Langton and Robbins (2007) offered,

> *OB considers that organizations are made up of individuals, groups and the entire organizational structure. Each of these units represents a different level within an organization, moving from the smallest unit, the individual, to the largest, the entire organization.* (p. 6)

Figure 4. The Organization Behavior Model

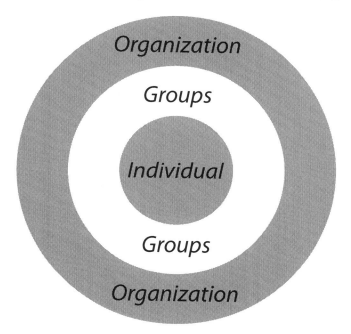

Individual Shifts for Individual Employees

Individual employees can claim their place at the table. Involving employees in the change initiative is critical to its overall success. Individual employees who take the time to familiarize themselves with William Bridges's (2003) transition model have tools for recognizing their individual transition responses and are in a stronger position to gain necessary support for themselves and their colleagues.

Shifts for Organizational Change Practitioners

As change practitioners, we need to consider three qualities that can strengthen change initiatives: curiosity, openness, and advocating. First is curiosity about the people, the process and the change. Too often, I witness organizations struggle with external consultants who have expertise but forget to listen to the client. Only through getting curious and listening deeply can we hope to appreciate the challenges, doubts, reservations, possibilities and opportunities that organizational leaders and their members are experiencing. Curiosity is also at the core of change offered by Storch (2015). He described the type of dialogic consulting required as including "the skills to stay in the moment with others, to engage their concerns and meaning making without providing answers or false certainty to assuage their anxiety about change, and to facilitate conversations that generate new possibilities are vital" (p. 204).

Second is the quality of openness. Staying open to input that may prompt shifts in understanding, planning and implementation, helps build strong collaborative relationships with the client. Also, having an open heart creates space for an empathic understanding of the client experience. Entering into change initiatives with an open heart deepens your understanding of what help you can offer.

Third, advocating for appropriate service for the organization and its employees becomes an important criterion for successfully navigating change using the 5C Model. As an external consultant, I often ask myself, "What intervention operates in service of the organization right now?" and "What does the organization need from me right now?" The answer to the second question may be "nothing"; perhaps the organization at this moment requires nothing from you. In our action-oriented world, doing nothing can be a challenge.

Finally, a passion for this work serves the client and the project. Whether you are an internal or external change practitioner, clients appreciate passion. However, the various stages of transition call for different approaches by leaders and change practitioners. The 5C Model is easy to share and lets practitioners step into dialogue with a client. It also helps the organization navigate change with a focus on success and integration.

The focus on curiosity, openness, advocacy, and passion are the fuel to support and increase collaboration. As I articulated earlier, no one navigates change alone. I pose the following key questions to change practitioners: Who are the untapped members of the organization that I can collaborate with in service of this change? Who could I be making requests of for support? Who could I join with that I haven't yet engaged in this initiative?

Shifts in the Role of Leadership

> The sooner leaders stop trying to be all things to all people, the better off their organizations will be.... Only when leaders come to see themselves as incomplete, having strengths and weaknesses, will they be able to make up for their missing skills.... Incomplete leaders differ from incompetent leaders in that they understand what they're good at and what they're not and have good judgment about how they can work with others to build on their strengths and offset their limitations. (Ancona, Malone, Orlikowski, & Senge, 2007, pp. 92–94)

The 5C Model calls on leaders to make significant shifts in their approach to their work. If, as a leader, you have assumed you were responsible for the success or failure of your organization, the shift needs to begin with you. To create a successful level of employee involvement and ownership, leaders must let go of the notion they have all the answers. In our increasingly complex world, no one person has all the answers. It's not sustainable. All too often in the private sector, the board and CEO place this burden on their senior leadership team. In the public sector, the public and media exert this pressure. The pressure is unrelenting and we yearn for answers to questions like, what ever happened to treating people as human beings who may not have the answer at their fingertips? Better yet, why are we talking to the leader instead of the person most directly responsible? Now there's a novel concept! What a great opportunity to build capacity among our people to represent us, rather than limiting them from speaking publicly.

Also, employees want to contribute and feel they have made a difference. As leaders, we do a disservice to our people and organizations if our desire to "be responsible" stunts the ability of our colleagues to grow, develop and contribute. There is nothing more discouraging than speaking with an employee who received significant funding for advanced education and professional development, and then failed to fully use their new skill to benefit their organization. When this happens, employees typically leave to work at an organization that wants their skill and talent.

People development is a key leadership opportunity. Anyone supervising someone pursuing an advanced education has the opportunity to hold quarterly discussions on what the individual is learning, and actively consider how it might translate into stretch assignments of benefit to the organization. This applies especially when there is an opportunity to partner with another department or business unit to ensure that the employee is granted developmental opportunities aligned with their new skills. Guard against treating advanced education as something employees do on their own time. Imagine the possibilities if we as leaders leverage that passion and talent in service of our organization's mission and vision.

The opportunities to use the 5C Model are endless for you, your people, and your organization. May this model offer assistance to you for changes you experience. It is simple but as we all know, simple doesn't always mean easy. Be vigilant when a voice in your head says, "It would be so much easier to do this myself." That's the voice of responsibility and expediency. As someone who is recovering from the illness of being "overly responsible" I have found it valuable to invest in people and their involvement throughout the process. Otherwise I risk lowering engagement and ownership, which is counterproductive to achieving employee-owned responsibility for the change. As leaders, we owe it to our people and ourselves to let go, and let our people grow.

Leadership, Letting go and the Ecocycle

As part of learning about how to let go and let the people around me grow, I have come to rely on the ecocycle as a tool to support my ongoing inquiry into this topic. The eco-cycle has a long history, and I was introduced to it through the work of Brenda Zimmerman. The ecocycle takes us through a journey of birth, growth, and maturity, and then suggests that creative destruction is required in order to move us through to renewal and rebirth. When I am seeking to cultivate opportunities for letting go, I ask myself what assumptions or mental models (Senge, 2006) might I be holding on to? For example, the idea that "this would be easier if I did it myself" would prevent me from fully leveraging the people around me in times of change.

There are several articles written on the ecocycle, such as Hurst and Zimmerman's (1994) examination of the use of the ecocycle. Their article adapts a model that came from ecology and applies it to human organizational environments. The model invites each of us, regardless of what human or natural system we find ourselves in, to continuously reflect on what actions we can take that will contribute to renewal. By using the ecocycle framework, the process of creative destruction highlights the need for us to be consistently examining what no longer serves us and our organizations. I appreciate this framework because it helps me to see what needs to shift, be transformed, let go, or otherwise removed in order for change in leaders and organizations to move forward. As Hurst and Zimmerman (1994) asserted, "[Managers] have to constructively destroy their organizations by breaking the constraints that bind them or challenging the implicit assumptions of the organization" (p. 352). The work of creative destruction contributes to a cyclical and ongoing process of renewal represented by the infinity loop of the ecocycle (see Figure 5).

Figure 5. . The Ecocycle Model

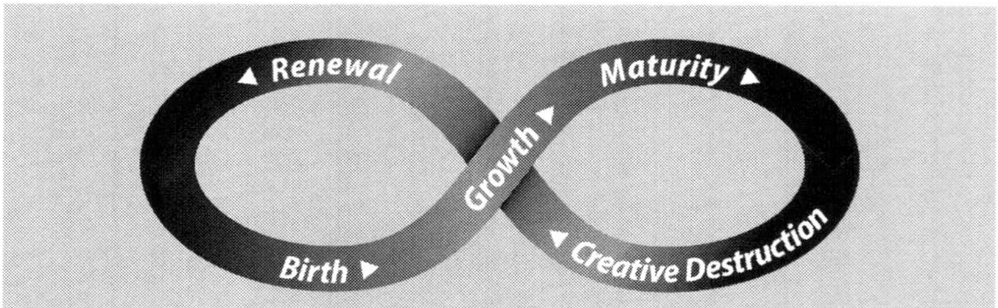

The ecocycle is also used in an alternative format as a liberating structure (Lipmanowicz & McCandless, 2014). See the Internet Resources section for a link to additional resources.

As you explore possible shifts called for in your leadership, ask yourself, "Where are the potential partners, collaborators and supporters who can help me?" and "What can I let go of to create opportunity for someone else?"

Change Leadership Sustainability and Values

What happens next matters, and one of the crucial opportunities for moving forward is to honor the scholarship, the history, and the leaders who provided the foundation for moving forward as we come together across disciplines to discover the both–and possibility for moving forward together. In essence, we have the opportunity to serve as bridges to more fully understand and integrate each other's efforts in service of the leaders of today and tomorrow.

In light of the last decade of the issues associated with leaders who operate within the dominant paradigm, what we do next matters. I want to nourish and contribute to the ongoing incubation of alternative values-based approaches to leadership so leaders can sustain themselves, their people, their organizations.

I am going to leave you with a passage from a poem written by June Jordan (1980) that she wrote for South African women. It says, "We are the ones we've been waiting for" (p. 43). If we are the ones we have been waiting for, our organizations and the people around us are in good hands.

I invite you to join me on this journey so that we can work together, because what happens next matters. Maybe we are the ones we've been waiting for, who can and indeed are making it happen as we use our gifts, our hearts, and our talents to make a contribution to values-based sustainable leaders, sustainable organizations, with sustainable people.

Conclusion – Values Release the Hero in Everyone

At the heart of the 5C framework for change are the values leaders hold dear. Values-based leadership is a lifelong journey of learning and discovery. This form of change leadership is noble and sacred work. I am struck by the possibilities that can emerge when leaders harness the wisdom in their people. The conclusion of this chapter came as I reflected on this comment from a research participant:

> *One of the reasons I appreciate this conversation is because it makes you think of things in a different way—but actually, as I said, it is about...assuming that there is sort of a hero in everybody and how do you bring that out.*

As I reflected on her words, I thought to myself, *'Values release the hero in everyone.'* This belief would offer an opportunity to build capacity in everyone particularly amidst change, to consider issues from the perspective of generating solutions and recommendations that operate within shared values. The 5C model calls for change leaders to embrace their values, become leaders of transition, support ongoing development of their own personal mastery, and sustain a strong personal and professional network. With these pillars in place, the opportunities to move beyond the heroic model of leadership to step into a future in which ongoing work on values in oneself and others allows the hero in everyone to be nurtured and released. Our children and future generations are relying on us to adopt a generative approach to leadership that can sustain us and our planet. If you were the one you were waiting for, what choice would you make today to enable this desired future?

Finally, particularly in times of change, maintaining a focus on relationships among organizational members is important. In their work, Westley, Patton, and Zimmerman (2006) highlighted the power of relationships within our complex environments: "The whole is different than the sum of the parts... In complex systems, relationships are key. Connections or relationships define how complex systems work; an organization is its relationships, not its flow chart" (p. 7). The work of change leadership is fueled by the relationships that exist among the individuals, groups, and teams that make up the organization. Expecting the organizational chart to provide the answers to how organizational members connect with each other is accurate. However, it also is an incomplete reflection of what actually happens.

Leadership Vignette

One Leader's Influence

Gilbert Neves, a workshop participant, shared this compelling story of one leader's influence on him as they navigated a significant change in their organization. The CEO, Roger Skillings, defined TRUST as "Trust, Respect, Understanding, Service and Truth–the last letter recognizing that everything needs to end with Truth."

The TRUST acronym was introduced at the very beginning of our change process. Our CEO communicated the vision for the change we needed to have, to ensure our competitive edge in the high-performance sport marketplace in Canada and worldwide. He emphasized that we were embarking on a journey of constant change over the coming years, and he wanted us to have our eyes wide open and trust each other. We would get there together if we followed and lived TRUST!

Our CEO modeled TRUST. He was tireless in building trust with each staff member, stakeholder and board member. He was very respectful in his communications even when things got very intense as major organizational change was unfolding and leadership issues arose. In my opinion, he was able to not only model the TRUST acronym as a change leader and CEO of the lead organization orchestrating the change, but he was able to use it to galvanize employees to dig deep and give it their all to ensure that the changes went through and that we maintained our momentum. There was lots of frank and open communication at all levels of the organization. The CEO delivered sensitive and confidential information with care; he ensured you understood what it meant – what your role and responsibility with this information was and he asked if we would assist him. He generously recognized the people who worked with him.

The impact on me was very profound. He demonstrated to me that when you embarked on major change you needed to have a set of principles to guide you, that you needed to communicate these principles often, that you had to model them even if it meant taking risks. If the principles were sound and you empowered employees with them, you would succeed. You needed to be very good at communicating and motivating people, and at times find creative and strategic ways to line up the "chess pieces" of the change. Above all, he demonstrated to me the power and influence of building and maintaining strong relationships with your employees, co-workers, direct reports, stakeholders and board members. Being authentic would dictate if you had staying power as a leader, and determined if you would be able to motivate an organization and its culture to make the change happen—and execute it well. Finally, when I first started working with our CEO, I was early in my professional career and learning about my leadership style. Working with and for this leader really helped me to identify my own leadership qualities

146

as a natural people leader, collaborator, relationship builder, and negotiator. I owe my gratitude not only to this leader but also to the TRUST acronym and set of principles he used during this change which occurred over a multi-year period.

Background note: Roger Skillings, former CEO of PacificSport Canadian Sport Centre, Victoria, British Columbia, and Canadian Sport Centre Pacific, shared that the TRUST acronym came from discussions with Walter Donald, the founder of The Executive Network Inc., a Human Resource company in Victoria.

Shifts in Groups, Teams and Departments

One key shift is to avoid viewing departments as independent entities. Duhigg (2016) captured the key lessons learned by Google in developing high-performance teams. The power of norms, specifically those that create psychological safety for members of groups and team to take risks, was viewed as important to developing teams that performed. In the absence of attending to the needs of groups and teams amidst change we risk creating a "we–they" orientation that prompts internal competition at the expense of the organization, not in service of it. There are many frameworks for looking at the organization as a whole. The 5C Model is one approach for developing a change plan that looks at the whole change and where to make the first and subsequent shifts.

We start the necessary shift when we lead from a place of curiosity about the impact of our change initiatives on the whole organization.

Shifts in the Organization

It is indeed possible to learn and co-create the organization we desire. We just need to move away from fear toward greater learning. It takes discipline to create space for becoming a learning organization. Organizations that wish to extend organizational learning and development should align themselves with the powerful work of Peter Senge. *In The Fifth Discipline*, Peter Senge (2006) articulated the five disciplines that contribute to a learning organization: personal mastery, developing a shared vision, mental models, team learning, and systems thinking. Organizations committed to learning are encouraged to learn more, to share, and to begin to use the language of the fifth discipline.

When we embrace the five disciplines of learning organizations, we embark on change. Fear diminishes when learning is the focus. Think of your past school experiences. Was learning facilitated when you were facing fear of failure? More typically, we learn from both successful and not so successful projects. As I articulated in Chapter 4, there are important shifts that occur as we consider the possibility of moving from "me to we" and "we to us." The shift from "me to we" happens when we attend to team and team dynamics. Perhaps the intentional application of the disciplines of the learning organization is another vehicle that can support us as we seek to make the shift from "we to us" with greater predictability within our organizations.

Conclusion

As I speak with colleagues about how the 5C Model shifts people's thinking in their life and work, they tell me that people can apply the model to many different situations beyond change. As I reflect on their input, what surfaces is that the 5C Model highlights a focus on our relationships amidst change. It also offers a practical, tangible way for people to navigate change in a way that honors relationships in life and in work.

When asked for my bottom-line definition of the five Cs, I reply:

Communication: Share what matters to you and people will listen.

Confidentiality: Honor people by listening and honoring the privacy of their doubts and concerns.

Cultural compatibility: Honor the values of the people first.

Courtship: Always maintain the spirit of invitation because courtship never ends.

Completion: Finish what you start.

I wish you success as you work with the 5C Model, and I encourage you to have fun, invest in your people and watch that investment yield better results with change. Ownership occurs when employees know they can co-create the change journey. In honoring people, you enable change that enhances organizational life.

Internet Resources

Communications

T.J. Larkin and Sandar (2006): visit http://www.larkin.biz/ publications.htm to request their free publication: Communicating Big Change Using Small Communication

Emotional Intelligence

Learning in Action Technologies: visit http://learninginaction.com/ publications_books.php to locate additional resources in emotional intelligence.

For additional information and resources on emotional intelligence, visit http://www.eiconsortium.org/

Leadership

James Kouzes and Barry Posner: http://www.leadershipchallenge.com

Liberating Structures

For more information visit: http://www.liberatingstructures.com/

Polarity Management

Polarity Management website and resources: http://www. polaritymanagement.com/ for books, training and articles.

Laura Harvell (n.d.). Her polarity management exercise is included in Chapter 4 and she can be contacted at: lauraharvell@mac.com

Teams

Businessballs: visit http://www.businessballs.com/ to access free learning and development resources.

World Café

Click here if you want to learn more: http://www.theworldcafe.com/key-concepts-resources/world-cafe-method/

Culture and Values Resources

Personal Values Assessment: https://www.valuescentre.com/tools-assessments/pva/

Learn more about Culture Transformation Tools: https://www.valuescentre.com/cultural-transformation/

Resilience Resources

R@W Website: https://workingwithresilience.com.au/

Kathryn McEwen: https://www.youtube.com/watch?v=YauAID5EahU

A 2020 article on Resilience for Coach Entrepreneurs: https://vicoaches.org/the-resilient-entrepreneur-count-yourself-into-your-coaching-business/

Additional Change Happens Resources

https://dreamcatcher-consulting.com/change-happens/

References

Allal-Chérif, O. (2017). Promoting and managing collaborative performance. *Strategic Direction*, 33(2), 33–35. https://dx.doi.org/10.1108/SD-11-2016-0149

Amar, A. D., Hentrich, C., & Hlupic, V. (2009). To be a better leader, give up authority. *Harvard Business Review*, 87(12), 22–24.

Ancona, D., Malone, T. W., Orlikowski, W. J., & Senge, P. M. (2007). In praise of the incomplete leader. *Harvard Business Review*, 85(2), 92–100.

Armson, R. (2011). *Growing wings on the way: Systems thinking for messy situations.* Devon, United Kingdom: Triarchy Press.

Barrett, R. (1998). *Liberating the corporate soul: Building a visionary organization.* Boston, MA: Butterworth-Heinemann.

Barrett, R. (2010). *The importance of values in high performance culture.* Retrieved from https://www.valuescentre.com/sites/default/files/uploads/2010-07-06/The%20Importance%20of%20Values.pdf

Barsh, J., Capozzi, M. M., & Davidson, J. (2008). Leadership and innovation. *McKinsey Quarterly*, *1*, 37–47. Retrieved from https://www.mckinsey.com/business-functions/strategy-and-corporate-finance/our-insights/leadership-and-innovation

Barwise, P., & Meehan, S. (2008). So you think you're a good listener. *Harvard Business Review*, 86 (4), 22.

Beckhard, R., & Harris, R. T. (1987). *Organizational transitions: Managing complex change.* Menlo Park, CA: Addison-Wesley.

Block, P. (2008). *Community: The structure of belonging.* San Francisco, CA: Berrett-Koehler.

Bolman, L. G., & Deal, T. E. (2008). *Reframing organizations: Artistry, choice and leadership*. San Francisco, CA: Jossey-Bass.

Bordas, J. (2012). *Salsa, soul and spirit: Leadership for a multicultural age*. San Francisco, CA: Berrett-Koehler.

Bridges, W. (2003). *Managing transitions: Making the most of change* (2nd ed.). Cambridge, MA: Da Capo Press.

Bridges, W. (2009). *Managing transitions: Making the most of change* (3rd ed.). Philadelphia, PA: Da Capo Press.

Bright, D. S., Cameron, K. S., & Caza, A. (2006). The amplifying and buffering effects of virtuousness in downsized organizations. *Journal of Business Ethics*, 64, 249–269. https://dx.doi.org/10.1007/s10551-005-5904-4

Brooks, A., & John, L. (2018). The surprising power of questions. *Harvard Business Review*, 96(3), 60–67.

Brown, B. (2015). *Rising strong: The reckoning. The rumble. The revolution*. New York, NY: Spiegel and Grau.

Brown, B. (2018). *Dare to lead: Brave work, tough conversations, whole hearts*. New York, NY: Random House.

Bungay Stanier, M. (2016). *The coaching habit: Say less, ask more & change the way you lead forever*. Toronto, Canada: Box of Crayons Press.

Buono, A. F., & Bowditch, J. L. (1989). *The human side of mergers and acquisitions: Managing collisions between people, cultures, and organizations*. San Francisco, CA: Jossey-Bass.

Buono, A. F., & Nurick, A. J. (1992). Intervening in the middle: Coping strategies in mergers and acquisitions. *Human Resource Planning*, 15(2), 19–33.

Bushe, G. R. (2001). *Clear leadership: How outstanding leaders make themselves understood, cut through the mush, and help everyone get real at work*. Mountain View, CA: Davies-Black.

Busch, T., & Wennes, G. (2012). Changing values in the modern public sector: The need for value-based leadership. *The International Journal of Leadership in Public Services, 8*(4), 201–215. https://dx.doi.org/10.1108/17479881211323599

Bushe, G. R., & Marshak, R. (Eds.). (2015). *Dialogic organization development: The theory and practice of transformational change.* Oakland, CA: Berrett-Koehler.

Cameron, K. (2011). Responsible leadership as virtuous leadership. *Journal of Business Ethics, 98*(Suppl. 1), 25–35. https://dx.doi.org/10.1007/s10551-011-1023-6

Conger, J. A. (1998). The necessary art of persuasion. *Harvard Business Review,* 76(3), 84–95.

Copeland, M. K. (2014). The emerging significance of values based leadership: A literature review. *International Journal of Leadership Studies,* 8, 105–135.

Darling, M., Parry, C., & Moore, J. (2005). Learning in the thick of it. *Harvard Business Review,* 83(7/8), 84–92.

De Kluyver, C. A., & Pearce, J. A., II. (2003). *Strategy: A view from the top: An executive perspective.* Upper Saddle River, NJ: Prentice Hall.

Denison, D. R. (1990). *Corporate culture and organizational effectiveness.* New York, NJ: John Wiley and Sons.

Devane, T. (2007). Sustainability of results. In P. Holman, T. Devane, & S. Cady (Eds.), *The change handbook: The definitive resource on today's best methods for engaging whole systems* (pp. 59–70). San Francisco, CA: Berrett-Koehler.

Diochon, M., & Anderson, A. R. (2011). Ambivalence and ambiguity in social enterprise: Narratives about values in reconciling purpose and practices. *International Entrepreneurship and Management Journal, 7,* 93–109. https://dx.doi.org/10.1007/s11365-010-0161-0

Duhigg, C. (2016). What Google learned from its quest to build the perfect team. *The New York Times Magazine*. Retrieved from https://www.nytimes.com/2016/02/28/magazine/what-google-learned-from-its-quest-to-build-the-perfect-team.html

Etmanski, C., Fulton, M., Nasmyth, G., & Page, M. B. (2014). The dance of joyful leadership. In K. Schuyler, J. Baugher, K. Jironet, & L. Lid-Falkman (Eds.), *Leading with spirit, presence, and authenticity* (pp. 91–108). San Francisco, CA: Jossey-Bass.

Ferdig, M. A. (2007). Sustainability leadership: Co-creating a sustainable future. *Journal of Change Management, 7*(1), 25–35. https://doi.org/10.1080/14697010701233809

Fletcher, J. K. (2012). The relational practice of leadership. In M. Uhl-Bien & S. M. Ospina (Eds.), *Advancing relational leadership research: A dialogue among perspectives* (pp. 83–106). Charlotte, NC: Information Age.

Frost, J. (2014). Values based leadership. *Industrial and Commercial Training, 46*, 124–129. https://dx.doi.org/10.1108/ICT-10-2013-0073

Galford, R., & Drapeau, A. S. (2003). The enemies of trust. *Harvard Business Review, 81*(2), 88–95.

George, B., Sims, P., McLean, A., & Mayer, D. (2007). Discovering your authentic leadership. *Harvard Business Review, 85*(2), 129–138.

George, W. (2004). Find your voice. In S. Clarke (Ed.), Leading by feel. *Harvard Business Review, 82*(1), 35.

Goldsmith, M., Govindarajan , V., Kaye, B., & Vicere, A. A. (2003). The many facets of leadership. Upper Saddle River, NJ: *Financial Times Prentice Hall.*

Goleman, D. (2004). Never stop learning. In S. Clarke (Ed.), *Leading by feel. Harvard Business Review, 82*(1), 28.

Greenleaf, R. K. (1998). *The power of servant leadership.* San Francisco, CA: Berrett-Koehler.

Greenleaf, R. K. (2008). *The servant as leader.* Westfield, IA: The Greenleaf Center for Servant Leadership.

Hall, B. P. (2001). Values development and learning organizations. *Journal of Knowledge Management*, 5(1), 19–32. https://dx.doi.org/10.1108/13673270110384374

Heifetz, R. (2004). Question authority. In S. Clarke (Ed.), Leading by feel. *Harvard Business Review*, 82(1), 37.

Heifetz, R. A., & Linsky, M. (2002). *Leadership on the line: Staying alive through the dangers of leading.* Boston, MA: Harvard Business School Press.

Holman, P., Devane, T., & Cady, S. (2007). *The change handbook: The definitive resource on today's best methods for engaging whole systems.* San Francisco, CA: Berrett-Koehler.

Hurst, D. K., & Zimmerman, B. J. (1994). From life cycle to ecocycle: A new perspective on the growth, maturity, destruction, and renewal of complex systems. *Journal of Management Inquiry*, 3(4), 339–354. https://doi.org/10.1177/105649269434008

Johnson, B. (1996). *Polarity management: Identifying and managing unsolvable problems.* Amherst, MA: Human Resource Development.

Johnson, B. (2003). *Polarity management: One tool for managing complexity and ambiguity.* In M. Goldsmith & V. Govindarajan (Eds.), The many facets of leadership (pp. 139–150). Upper Saddle River, NJ: Pearson.

Johnson, J. (2010). *EQ fitness handbook – you in relationship – 300 daily practices to build EQ fitness.* Bellevue, WA: Learning in Action Technologies.

Jordan, J. (1980). *Passion: New poems*, 1977–1980. Boston, MA: Beacon Press.

Kahane, A. (2010). *Power and love: A theory and practice of social change.* San Francisco, CA: Berrett-Koehler.

Kenny, C. (2012). Liberating leadership theory. In C. Kenny & T. Ngaroimata Fraser (Eds.), *Living Indigenous leadership: Native narratives on building strong communities* (pp. 1–17). Vancouver, Canada: UBC Press.

Kerber, K., & Buono, A. (2018). The rhythm of change leadership. *Organization Development Journal*, 36(3), 55–72.

Kiel, F. (2015). *Return on character: The real reason leaders and their companies win.* Boston, MA: Harvard Business Review Press.

Kirk, P., & Shutte, A. M. (2004). Community leadership development. *Community Development Journal*, 39, 234–251. https://dx.doi.org/10.1093/cdj/bsh019

Koestenbaum, P. (2003). Facing the paradoxes of leadership: Eight rules. In M. Goldsmith & V. Govindarajan (Eds.), *The many facets of leadership* (pp. 151–156). Upper Saddle River, NJ: Pearson.

Kotter, J. P. (1996). *Leading change.* Boston, MA: Harvard Business School Press.

Kotter, J. P., & Cohen, D. S. (2002). *The heart of change: Real-life stories of how people change their organizations.* Boston, MA: Harvard Business School Press.

Kouzes, J. M., & Posner, B. Z. (2003). *The leadership challenge* (3rd ed.). San Francisco, CA: Jossey-Bass.

Kouzes, J. M., & Posner, B. Z. (2007). *The Leadership Challenge* (4th ed.). San Francisco, CA: Jossey-Bass.

Kralik, D., Visentin, K., & Van Loon, A. (2006). Transition: A literature review. *Journal of Advanced Nursing,* 55(3), 320–329. https://dx.doi.org/10.1111/j.1365-2648.2006.03899.x

Kwan, L. (2019). The collaboration blind spot. *Harvard Business Review*, 97(2), 66–73. Langton, S. P., & Robbins, N. (2007). *Organizational behaviour concepts, controversies, applications.* Toronto, Canada: Pearson–Prentice Hall.

Lalich, J. (2004). Watch your culture. In S. Clarke (Ed.), Leading by feel. *Harvard Business Review*, 82(1), 34.

Larkin, T. J., & Larkin, S. (2006). Communicating big change using small communication. Retrieved from http://www.larkin.biz/data/Communicating_Big_Change-English.pdf

Larson, C. L., & Murtadha, K. (2002). Leadership for social justice. *Yearbook of the National Society for the Study of Education*, 101(1), 134–161. https://dx.doi.org/10.1111/j.1744-7984.2002.tb00007.x

Larson, D. E., & Hunter, J. E. (2014). Separating wheat from chaff: How secondary school principals' core values and beliefs influence decision-making related to mandates. *NCPEA International Journal of Educational Leadership Preparation, 9*(2), 71–90.

Lipmanowicz, H., & McCandless, K. (2016). *The surprising power of liberating structures: Simple rules to unleash a culture of innovation.* Seattle, WA: Liberating Structures Press.

Maister, D. H., Green, C. H., & Galford, R. M. (2000). *The trusted advisor.* New York, NY: Simon & Schuster.

Manz, C. C., Anand, V., Joshi, M., & Manz, K. P. (2008). Emerging paradoxes in executive leadership: A theoretical interpretation of the tensions between corruption and virtuous values. *The Leadership Quarterly*, 19(3), 385–392. https://dx.doi.org/10.1016/j.leaqua.2008.03.009

McEwen, K. (2016). *Building your resilience: How to thrive in a challenging job*. St. Marys, Australia: Openbook Howden Print & Design.

Meadows, D. (2008). *Thinking in systems: A primer*. White River Junction, VT: Chelsea Green.

Meglino, B. M., & Ravlin, E. C. (1998). *Individual values in organizations: Concepts, controversies, and research*. Journal of Management, 24, 351–389. doi:10.1177/014920639802400304

Morgan, N. (2008). How to become an authentic speaker. *Harvard Business Review*, 86(1), 115–119.

Noer, D. M. (1993). *Healing the wounds: Overcoming the trauma of layoffs and revitalizing downsized organizations*. San Francisco, CA: Jossey-Bass.

Nohria, N., Groysberg, B., & Lee, L.-E. (2008). Employee motivation: A powerful new model. *Harvard Business Review*, 86(7/8), 78–84.

Ospina, S. M., & Sorenson, G. L. J. (2006). A constructionist lens on leadership: Charting new territory. In G. R. Goethals & G. L. J. Sorenson (Eds.), *The quest for a general theory of leadership* (pp. 188–204). Northampton, MA: Edward Elgar.

O'Toole, J. (1996). *Leading change: The argument for values-based leadership*. New York, NY: Ballantine Books.

Paarlberg, L. E., & Perry, J. L. (2007). Values management: Aligning employee values and organization goals. *The American Review of Public Administration*, 37, 387–408. https://dx.doi.org/10.1177/0275074006297238

Page, M. B. (2006). *Done deal: Your guide to merger and acquisition integration*. Victoria, Canada: Authenticity Press.

Page, M. B. (2016). Public leadership: Navigating leadership challenges and operating in service of the common good in an interconnected world. *International Journal of Public Leadership*, 12(2), 112–128. https://dx.doi.org/10.1108/IJPL-12-2015-0030

Page, M. B., & Margolis, R. (2017). Cocreating collaborative learning environments using adult learning principles in the classroom. In C. Etmanski, K. Bishop, & M. B. Page (Eds.), *Adult learning through collaborative leadership* (pp. 77–88). San Francisco, CA: Jossey-Bass.

Posner, B. Z., Kouzes, J. M., & Schmidt, W. H. (1985). Shared values make a difference: An empirical test of corporate culture. *Human Resource Management*, 24, 293–309. https://dx.doi.org/10.1002/hrm.3930240305

Raelin, J. (2018). Learning your way out. *Chief Learning Officer*, 17(3). Retrieved from https://www.chieflearningofficer.com/2018/03/21/learning-your-way-out/

Rogerson, S., Meir, R., Crowley-McHattan, Z., McEwen, K., & Pastoors, R. (2016). A randomized controlled pilot trial investigating the impact of a workplace resilience program during a time of significant organizational change. *Journal of Occupational and Environmental Medicine*, 58(4), 329–334. https://dx.doi.org/10.1097/JOM.0000000000000677

Ruiz, D. M. (1997). *The four agreements: A practical guide to personal freedom, a Toltec wisdom book*. San Rafael, CA: Amber-Allen.

Rusaw, C. (2005). A proposed model of feminist public sector leadership. *Administrative Theory & Praxis*, 27(2), 385–393.

Russell, R. F. (2001). The role of values in servant leadership. *Leadership & Organization Development Journal*, 22, 76–84. https://dx.doi.org/10.1108/01437730110382631

Ryan, K. D., & Oestreich, D. K. (1998). *Driving fear out of the workplace: Creating the high-trust, high-performance organization*. San Francisco, CA: Jossey-Bass.

Salovey, P., & Mayer, J. D. (1990). Emotional intelligence. *Imagination, Cognition, and Personality, 9,* 185–211. https://dx.doi.org/10.2190/DUGG-P24E-52WK-6CDG

Scanlon, J. (2008, April 28). How to make meetings matter. *Business Week Online.* Retrieved from https://www.bloomberg.com/news/articles/2008-04-28/how-to-make-meetings-matterbusinessweek-business-news-stock-market-and-financial-advice

Schein, E. H. (1983). *Organizational culture: A dynamic model* (Report TR-ONR-13). Retrieved from http://dspace.mit.edu/bitstream/handle/1721.1/48689/organizationalcu00sche.pdf?sequence=1

Schein, E. H. (1984). Coming to a new awareness of organizational culture. *Sloan Management Review, 25*(2), 3–16.

Schein, E. H. (1992). *Organizational culture and leadership* (2nd ed.). San Francisco, CA: Jossey-Bass.

Scott, S. (2002). *Fierce conversations: Achieving success at work & in life, One conversation at a time.* New York, NY: Berkley.

Secretan, L. H. K. (1999). *Inspirational leadership: Destiny, calling and cause.* Toronto, Canada: Macmillan.

Secretan, L. H. K. (2010). *The spark, the flame and the torch: Inspire self. Inspire others. Inspire the world.* Caledon, Ontario: The Secretan Center.

Senge, P. M. (2006). *The fifth discipline: The art & practice of the learning organization.* New York, NY: Currency Doubleday.

Short, R. R. (1998). *Learning in relationship: Foundation for personal and professional success.* Bellevue, WA: Learning in Action Technologies.

Short, R. R. (2005). *The eye of "I" – The evolution to first-person social science* (Unpublished manuscript). Bellevue, WA: Learning in Action Technologies.

Stallard, M. L., & Pankau, J. (2008). Strengthening human value in organizational cultures. *Leader to Leader, 2008*(47), 18–23. https://doi.org/10.1002/ltl.264

Sinclair, A. (2007). *Leadership for the disillusioned: Moving beyond myths and heroes to leading that liberates*. Crows Nest, Australia: Allen and Unwin.

Sinclair, A. (2009). Seducing leadership: Stories from leadership development. *Gender, Work and Organization, 16*(2), 266–284. https://dx.doi.org/10.1111/j.1468-0432.2009.00441.x

Sipe, J. W., & Frick, D. M. (2009). *The seven pillars of servant leadership: Practicing the wisdom of leading by serving*. Mahwah, NJ: Paulist Press.

Spears, L. C. (2002). The understanding and practice of servant-leadership. In L. Spears & M. Lawrence (Eds.), Practicing servant-leadership: Succeeding through trust, bravery, and forgiveness (pp. 9–24). Indianapolis, IN: The Greenleaf Center for Servant-Leadership.

Spears, L. C., & Lawrence, M. (2004). Love and work: A conversation with James A. Autry. In L. C. Spears & M. Lawrence (Eds.), *Practicing servant leadership: Succeeding through trust, bravery, and forgiveness* (pp. 47–69). San Francisco, CA: Jossey-Bass.

Stone, D., Patton, B., & Heen. S. (1999). *Difficult conversations: How to discuss what matters most*. New York, NY: Penguin Group.

Storch, J. (2015). Enabling change: The dialogic skills of OD. In G. Bushe, & R. Marshak (Eds.), *Dialogic organization development: The theory and practice of transformational change* (pp. 197–218). Oakland, CA: Berrett-Koehler.

Ungar, M. (2019, May 25). Put down the self-help books. Resilience is not a DIY endeavor. *The Globe and Mail*. Retrieved from https://www.theglobeandmail.com/opinion/article-put-down-the-self-help-books-resilience-is-not-a-diy-endeavour/

Van Wart, M. (1998). *Changing public sector values*. New York, NY: Garland Publishing.

Van Wart, M. (2014). Contemporary varieties of ethical leadership in organizations. *International Journal of Business Administration, 5*(5), 27–45. https://dx.doi.org/10.5430/ijba.v5n5p27

Wagamese, R. (2016). *Embers: One Ojibway's meditations.* Madeira Park, Canada: Douglas and McIntyre.

Watkins, M. (2013). *The first 90 days: Proven strategies for getting up to speed faster and smarter.* Boston, MA: Harvard Business School Press.

Waugh, B. (with Forrest, M. S.). (2001). *The soul in the computer: The story of a corporate revolutionary.* Maui, HI: Inner Ocean.

Webb, K. S. (2009). Why emotional intelligence should matter to management: A survey of the literature. *SAM Advanced Management Journal,* 32–41.

Westley, F., Patton, M., & Zimmerman, B. (2006). *Getting to maybe: How the world is changed.* Toronto, Canada: Random House Canada.

Wheatley, M. J. (2005). *Finding our way: Leadership for an uncertain time.* San Francisco, CA: Berrett-Koehler.

Wheatley, M. J. (2009). *Are we all in this together?* Retrieved from http://www.margaretwheatley.com/articles/All-In-This-Together.pdf

Wood Daudelin, M. (1996). Learning from experience through reflection. *Organizational Dynamics, 24*(3), 36–48. https://dx.doi.org/10.1016/S0090-2616(96)90004-2

Worley, C. G., Hitchin, D. E., & Ross, W. L. (1996). *Integrated strategic change: How organizational development builds competitive advantage.* Menlo Park, CA: Addison-Wesley.

Young Leon, A. (2012). Elders' teachings on leadership: Leadership as gift. In C. Kenny & T. Ngaroimata Fraser (Eds.), *Living Indigenous leadership: Native narratives on building strong communities* (pp. 48–63). Vancouver, Canada: UBC Press.

Learn More about Change

For more information about change management and Beth Page's speaking, coaching and consulting services, go to the website at **www.dreamcatcher-consulting.com**

For change management resources, visit **www.dreamcatcher-consulting.com** to subscribe to *Dreamcatchers*, a monthly change management newsletter with tools, tips, book recommendations and exercises.

Buy the Book:

You may purchase *Change Happens: Your Guide to Navigating Change Using the 5C Model* or *Done Deal: Your Guide to Merger and Acquisition Integration* online at **www.authenticitypress.com.** Discounts are available for volume purchases.

Your Comments:

Feel free to email Beth your comments about this book. She can be contacted at **beth@dreamcatcher-consulting.com**

Websites for more information:

www.dreamcatcher-consulting.com
www.authenticitypress.com
www.mbethpage.com

Order More Books

Amazon.com carries both kindle and hard copies of all books published by Authenticity Press.

By mail: Authenticity Press
Suite 554, 185-911 Yates Street
Victoria, BC, V8V 4Y9

For more information visit: **www.authenticitypress.com**
Email orders: orders@authenticitypress.com
By phone: 844-483-6729

Change Happens:
Your Guide to Navigating Change
Using the 5C Model

Manufactured by Amazon.ca
Bolton, ON